ASSARACUS

A Journal of Gay Poetry
Issue 08

Alexander, Arkansas
www.siblingrivalrypress.com

Assaracus
A Journal of Gay Poetry
Issue 8: Fall 2012
ISBN: 978-1-937420-28-4
ISSN: 2159-0478
Bryan Borland, Editor
Seth Pennington, Associate Editor
Philip F. Clark, Art Editor
Copyright © 2012 by Sibling Rivalry Press

Cover Art: The Embrace by Noel Dean Doss. Used by Permission.

This issue of *Assaracus* is dedicated to D. Gilson, whose chapbook, *Catch & Release*, is available from Seven Kitchens Press. *The boys are the boys they want to be tonight. This is no accident of birth.*

All rights reserved. No part of this journal may be reproduced or republished without written consent from the publisher, except by reviewers who may quote brief excerpts in connection with a review in a newspaper, magazine, or electronic publication; nor may any part of this journal be reproduced, stored in a retrieval system, or transmitted in any form without written consent of the publisher. However, contributors maintain ownership rights of their individual poems and as such retain all rights to publish and republish their work.

Sibling Rivalry Press, LLC
13913 Magnolia Glen Drive
Alexander, AR 72002

www.siblingrivalrypress.com
info@siblingrivalrypress.com

Assaracus Issue 08

The Poems of John Barton
p. 7

The Poems of Walter Beck
p. 15

The Poems of Charlie Bondhus
p. 26

The Poems of Allen F. Clark
p. 41

The Poems of Nick Comilla
p. 57

The Poems of Jim Cory
p. 68

The Poems of Carlton Fisher
p. 77

The Poems of Edmund Miller
p. 87

The Poems of Joseph Rathgeber
p. 97

The Poems of Bill Trüb
p. 107

The Poems of Steve Turtell
p. 117

The Poems of Ocean Vuong
p. 125

Featuring the Art of Noel Dean Doss
Artist's Biography p. 136

JOHN BARTON

ONE BEDROOM APARTMENT

JOHN BARTON has published ten books of poetry and six chapbooks, including *Great Men* (Quarry, 1990), *Designs from the Interior* (Anansi, 1994), *Sweet Ellipsis* (ECW, 1998), *Hypothesis* (Anansi, 2001), *Asymmetries* (Frog Hollow, 2004), and *Hymn* (Brick, 2009). He also co-edited *Seminal: The Anthology of Canadian Gay Male Poets* for Arsenal Pulp in 2007. Selected poems, *For the Boy with the Eyes of the Virgin*, and a limited-edition chapbook, *Balletomane: The Program Notes of Lincoln Kirstein*, appeared respectively from Nightwood Editions and JackPine Press in 2012. He lives in Victoria, Canada, where he is the editor of *The Malahat Review*.

www.malahatreview.ca

John Barton

ONE BEDROOM APARTMENT

"For still temptation follows where thou art."
Sonnet 41, William Shakespeare

I

What Tempest Within

Unlooked-for flash—
                    the flesh, a room revealed
by lightning not misunderstood as fire
but sound. The rain was thunder, never ire
as nails it drove in hard through shingles sealed
against entry, those little tongues of steeled
disaster you and I could not aspire
to turning sharp away from, bloodless, tire
us still, unthoughtful one-night love
                                    —annealed.

The dulling storm undulls the cooling brain.

We lie apart, unspent and silent, loud
with words unmouthed, our bodies' residue
unsafe evaporating slicks that stain
not just the arid sheets but skins, our shroud
of vapid sweat from which unfeeling flew.

II

From a Portfolio of Japanese Erotic Prints

Of vapid sweat from which unfeeling flew
you blow me slow, attentive eyes not shut
so jarred, I jerk awake at once, your blue
unquestioned stare inclined to move from nut

to hip, its line inscribed in spry woodcut
metrics up my torso to lips and brow
till I can't turn my gaze from yours, my butt
ensnared in dampened linens, cracked window

agape behind your head—a jack-pine bough
averse with wet it shakes through summer screens
in place beyond the snows, I note, till now—
unloosed by gales—the way my body leans

inside your own, a woodcut graven fresh
of men not prone to spoon, who fast enmesh.

III

Maj. Tom's Cyberspace Oddity

Of men not prone to spoon, who fast enmesh
I know not one with eyes as frank as yours
remorseless guys who come online, not flesh

but gigabytes; each .gif they post downpours
a faceless shard of fuzzy body parts
through clouds of RAM, as, lost, it meteors

a falling asteroid of REM to chart
deleted longing. Mine, theirs—who would care?
Such veiled chance trajectories none imparts

with thought, all inner space a haze of rare
and rude replies or worse: utter dead air—
empathic vacuums far from debonair

until your squirt of queries coursed with flair—
your sleeve rolled up, my tattooed heart aware.

IV

Peter Fonda and Me

Your sleeve rolled up, my tattooed heart aware—
with opened eyes we know what skin may tell
if nothing else. Our engines, revving, blare
essential anguish, rank desire, such hell
the freedom we discharge as bikers jacked
before we join, angst blown off as hapless
roadkill, tongues hit then run, detouring tact
two men without aim who ride helmetless

just as the big easy gushes down, comes
to ground, every belvedere a plateau
where prairie snarled as rucked-up sheets succumbs
to flat horizon, scrub unfurled below
once scored by ecstasy, the skid we leave
careless transcript too injurious to grieve.

V

Cavafy's Blinds, An Hour Open

Careless transcript injurious to grieve
I scan your back before you dress, its pores

erased from dawn's recall, the airy sleeve
of night you wore now torn by what restores

ennui with raised-up blinds, to flood naive
through sheers my tuneless solitude abhors—

abs etched like yours about to find reprieve
from white, still drying inks my tongue adores

but no longer tastes, clothes re-zipped on, bed
half made, the ceiling's gloom a sheet unshaped

by unsubtle forms as you leave, my head
void of future undreamt-of guests inscaped

as blanks, as I am blank, your likeness fled
and me not clear if light or shade's escaped.

VI

Donne In

And me not clear if light or shade's escaped
the crown you deigned to wear a cock-eyed ring
you, flaccid, slipped wholly free of, its sting
righteous STDs; false transcendence shaped
without regret, my gifts unwanted, scraped
from thighs despite our short-lived fantasies.
Unholy pipe dreams of which neither breathes
a word—our acts persist: they might be taped.

Or has perversion jaundiced me?
                                        Who lifts
my yellowed soul from unchanged sheets no one
lies in once I've rolled away from spendthrift's
unmeaning spray? Our pouring forth has done
me in; no one I care for states his name—

may no lust left unlaundered soak up blame.

VII

Like Crane's Heart, Abridged

May no lust left unlaundered soak up blame.

The paling dawn's washed clean the leaves outside
my window as midnight's street lamps subside
the day brisk as you stroll away, your frame
seamless against cloudbursts about to claim
reflection, your unlooking eyes at sea
in me—or did you turn to raise, in free
harbour, your hand and wave? Our span no shame
if brief.
              Two men dock and ghost cities form
from Brooklyn past Lion's Gate (joy concealed
by traffic), the charged tides below not warm
ships cast about, ache slipping anchor healed
in bunks by wireless pixellated storm—
unlooked-for flash
                    the flesh
                                a room revealed.

WALTER BECK

BE BRAVE

WALTER BECK is a poet from Avon, Indiana. He graduated from Indiana State University in Terre Haute with a BS in English and made a name for himself in the emerging Terre Haute poetry scene with his intense and shocking live performances often featuring blood, make-up, and semi-drag. Walter's work has been featured in a wide array of publications including *Burner, The ISU Tonic, Paradigm, Camp Chase Gazette, A Brilliant Record, Yes Poetry, The Q Review, Off the Rocks*, and others. He has independently released three albums of his live performances and has recently released his first chapbook, *Life Through Broken Pens*, available from Writing Knights Press. Love and hate mail can be sent to wtblackdeath@yahoo.com.

www.passedoutfullyclothed.blogspot.com

HOPES OF A YOUNG AMERICAN POET

I want poetry to be reborn in this country.
I want poetry out of the halls of academia
And back on the streets.

I want it dripping
Not just from the tongues of professors,
But from the tongues of people;
Ordinary people,
Unusual people,
Young people,
Old people,
In-the-middle people.

I want it scribbled
Not just in notebooks,
But in public bathroom stalls,
Carved into the sides of park benches,
Spray-painted on back alley walls.

I want people
Spitting not just old verse
That they remember from so long ago,
But new verse;
Coming alive from new poets,
Famous poets,
Underground poets,
I want people spitting their own verse.

I want to see
A thousand open-mic nights,
In a thousand different cities;
First-timers,
New-timers,
Long-timers,
Standing up
And sharing poetry
With the zeal and lust
Of hellfire preachers
And angry rioters.

I want poetry to be alive and dangerous again.

CONSOLATION PRIZE

Don't parade out your endless stream of pretty boys
And tell me I have a face.
Don't play your polished pop songs
And tell me I have a voice.
Don't give me your bureaucratic bullshit
And tell me I can stand up.

Don't wave your consolation prize
And tell me it's equality.

My face
Is in a parade of freaks.
My voice
Is in the ragged guitar of queercore.
I stand up
With a flag in a raised fist.

Don't wave your consolation prize
And tell me it's equality.

I am found
In the writings of William S. Burroughs.
I am found
In a Rocky Horror crowd.
I am found
In the reels of John Waters.

Don't wave your consolation prize
And tell me it's equality.

ANOTHER CLICHÉD LOVE POEM

I could write like all the others;
Speak of unrequited love,
Of those who weren't interested,
Those who were snatched late at night,
Or those who simply got away.

But it still wouldn't cure my blue balls.

I'd rather write of the love I have;
Of new territories,
Awaking the muse in those who never thought he existed,
Or the reporters sticking their mics and pens
In my face,
Knowing I would give them the defiant babble
They craved.

It can be love from a distance,
But through beery, smoky eyes
It's enough for me.

Walter Beck

IT'S LIKE GIVING ROSES FOR A WRITER

Walking off the stage;
After the longest set of my career,
Forty-five minutes,
Spitting romance and revolution
To half a dozen people,
Plus the sound guy.

But it doesn't matter;
It was new ground broken
And I felt alive.

I ran into you
After I walked off stage,
Still high from the performance
And about a dozen beers.

You only heard part of my diatribe on stage
Because you were getting ready
For your own show;
Holy Christ, you were beautiful
To my boozy, poetic eyes.

I gave you my set-list
So you could read it for yourself;

It was the closest thing
To a romantic gesture
I've ever really done.

(AIN'T NOBODY) BETTER THAN YOU

Professors pump you full of theory;
They want you to write
Like *The New Yorker*,
Even if you find the label on the bottle of Wild Irish Rose
To be more honest and beautiful
Than that canned shit.

And the students march the same line;
Repeating gibberish of criticism and form,
Shredding a story
Just like they were trained to.

The street preachers,
Who never preached a lick of love,
Will drag you down and break your spirit
Just so you'll either punch them
Or look up at them with weepy eyes
And say, "Yes, yes, you were right.
I'm a wretched person."

You can almost see them get a hard-on,
Or whatever passes for it
In their guilt-soaked world.
If I'm going to satisfy a sadist,
It'll be in the bedroom.

Even a fellow activist will drag you down,
If you don't non-conform
On the same level they do;
They'll still spit in your face,
Call you pretentious
As they become more splintered.

Editors are the strange lot,
The ones you have to watch for,
They'll break your spirit
Quicker than any of the above
With a string of rejection letters
You can braid and tie just right
To lynch your dreams.

They all think they're better
Than you.

UNREAD POEMS (FOR MY OLD MAN)

When I first started writing seriously,
Starting walking around with a notebook
Or a chapbook,
My old man told me
He used to write poetry.

He used to write poetry
When he was younger,
Before my brother and I
Were even thought of.

He spoke of Shakespeare,
Edgar Alan Poe,
And Robert Frost,
Who was his favorite.

He bought me a copy of "Howl"
And collections of Bukowski,
Poe, and Eliot.

I asked him
Whatever happened to his poetry.
He said it was buried in the attic
Or at grandma's.

Late at night
Away from the stage,
I wonder
What sort of poet my old man was.

I AM MORE THAN A COCKSUCKER
For Jack Smith

I am more than a cocksucker;
In fact, cocksucking or getting mine sucked
Is a very small part of my life.

Who I love
Is not the whole person,
It is one small slice of me.

You might as well paint my entire person
On something like
My brownish blond hair,
Or my pale blue eyes
(Just like the Lou Reed song).
How about my cigarette brand of choice
Or my tendency to go barefoot in public?

How about my job as a camp counselor
Or my stash of live bootlegged records?
Why not judge me
For my rainbow suspenders
Or my black beret?

After all,
These are no more important or descriptive
Than being a cocksucker.

If you must describe me based on one characteristic,
Spit "Poet!" in my face.

WHO ARE YOU DANCING FOR?

It's addictive as hell;
The headlines, the sidelines,
Having a pen or mic
Thrust in your face.

Christ, it's addictive;
And I ain't even famous,
Just a small-time loudmouth
Dancing for peanuts
For the local rags.

A Bible Brother rubbed it in my face
Quoting Dylan at me,
"You gotta serve somebody."
I thought I danced
For no man.

But it's so smooth and easy
To slip into that old skin;
Be the angry young man
Just one more time,
Clench your fist and wave your sign
Just one more time,
Get your headlines and color photo
Just one more time.

They hawk a few more papers
With your name splashed across them,
A local celebrity, a famous rabble-rouser.

But do they take you seriously
Anymore?
Did they ever take you seriously?
On the streets, in the papers,
Even on the stage
Did they ever take you seriously?
Did anyone?

Sometimes
It ain't so bad being used;
And sometimes
It's the rude awakening
You've been needing.

NATIONAL COMING OUT DAY 2011

For the first time
I didn't avoid the question
"Would you like your picture taken?"

Ten months ago
I burned down a cage
Of eight years,
Smashed and burned
The closet down
And lighting my cigarette
On the smoldering embers.

No I didn't avoid the question,
Held a sign high and proud,
"Bisexual,"
In my rainbow braces
And black beret,
Battered jeans
And my Eyehategod shirt.

Ten months
And a long walk since
Always waiting for the other shoe
To drop,
To flush years of work
Down.

She snapped the picture
With my rock n roll grin,
Headphones barking out
Jon Ginoli's "Anthem."

Am I committing career suicide
With one snap of a camera?
Other brothers and sisters
Who've served with me
Still in their own private hells,
Afraid to lose it all.

I gave her my email
To send me a copy of the picture
So I could show it

To the whole damn world.

Looking out that charred door;
Liberty?
Freedom?
Destruction?

The law commands me to be brave.

WHO ARE THESE WORDS FOR?

I read in the introduction to *Queer*
That Burroughs wrote it
For an audience of one.

That made me think;
How many of these
Are written for an audience
Of one?

Over the last six years
How many of these,
Full of nicknames, jargon
And inside jokes,
Are for the masses?

I know those editors,
Who flip through these
From time to time,
Don't see everything
Between the stanzas.

But isn't that the way
It should be?
If I wrote for the masses
The words lose their magic
In a mess of clichés and generalizations.

If I write for an audience of one;
Be it one person,
One place,
Or even one organization
I am more honest.

And isn't that what poetry is supposed to be?

CHARLIE BONDHUS

WALT SLIPPED A RING ON MY FINGER

CHARLIE BONDHUS has published two books of poetry—*What We Have Learned to Love*, which won Brickhouse Books' 2008-2009 Stonewall Competition, and *How the Boy Might See It* (Pecan Grove Press, 2009) which was a finalist for the 2007 Blue Light Press First Book Award. He has also published a gayish novella, *Monsters and Victims* (Gothic Press, 2010). His poetry appears in numerous periodicals, including *The Yale Journal for the Humanities in Medicine*, *The Tulane Review*, *Grey Sparrow Journal*, *The Q Review*, *Stone Telling*, *The SN Review*, and others. He holds an MFA in creative writing from Goddard College and a Ph.D. in literature from the University of Massachusetts, Amherst. He teaches at Raritan Valley Community College in New Jersey.

Charlie Bondhus

LETTER TO A BOY ON HIS TWENTY-FIRST BIRTHDAY

Hey Boy,

Twenty-one years old and you're
pretty much on schedule; lost some-
where between the leather and the lining-
cotton, unsure whether to insert an "i" or
a "u" between the "b" and the "tch."

Nervous lips descended
past a few hairless navels in
July's backseat,
tremoring hands and
heart built walls around a couple of
one- or two-time lovers, all of whom got
scared and climbed
the facade, like East Berlin refugees,
though the barbed wire on top actually tore your
flesh rather than theirs and the lashings,
like leather and thorn,
secured your belief that you are somehow
messianic; Jesus or not, you
must learn that

personal poetry will end badly;
consider instead the way the sun batters the
snow on a partly cloudy day, and,
if in that you see
a lover's treachery,
encode it.

Fantasizing will end badly;
instead, throw yourself
with all the unrestraint of one who is sleepwalking
into the day, and,
if in the process you behold his body,
embrace it.

Seeking love will end badly;
instead, remain open to naked experience—
the man on the street with the

hole in his jeans may not be the
boogeyman your parents and
teachers make him to be,
and, if in his arms you find
support,
return it,
though without flowers, wine, or kisses.

It was a real
treat to hear from you
seeing that the last time
we met was August at the lake,
and your parents and sisters and
the dog were there

so I couldn't really tell you how
I had decoded that ridiculous riddle
you had assembled in trimmed
chest hair, tight swim trunks, and hands lifted
at the wrist,
diving off the dock, slipshod, laughing
like a girl half your age,
turning in the
layered water with all the lethargy of
a roast on a spit.

Clean off of Christianity,
I'm sure you're familiar with the
Israelites' sin in
the desert, how,
frustrated, they built an
icon of
gold, so that they would have
something to kneel
before, trading gods as easily as
some boys trade secrets;
the moral being
that if you pile on "thou shalt and
shalt nots," they're gonna fall on
their knees in front of the first pretty
piece they see.

The soundest bit I can give you is
—whether naked or clothed—
to find his cheek

in a dark room
using only
your own, for,
when your stubble
meshes with his
(and there is always some),
the trappings of gender
-the kissing and being kissed,
the cock, the asshole, the mouth—
flee helter-skelter,
leaving simply
two men
who
love
other
men.

TEMPLE

Metal and vinyl clanged into monoliths
to which we chain
savage arms with their slurred russet
grease and reek. Quintessence of tissue,
the ocher of coals, he
grunts,
clangs again, knowing
what falls into place ought not
fall, but be
fought to rest
like the approach of death.
Something desired
by the faithful, those
cartwheels of light and wispy bits of
sculpture, wings and beauty, all of it being
—for us anyway—
something far more sarcous
and sheened, a lamina of
shimmer, like boulders at
sunset after high tide.

Here we are all men
with one object.

Charlie Bondhus

AN EQUIVOCAL LOVE

But the very man who should make attempts on a boy of twenty seems to me to be unnaturally lustful and pursuing an equivocal love. For then the limbs, being large and manly, are hard, the chins that once were soft are rough and covered with bristles, and the well-developed thighs are as it were sullied with hairs.
- Lucian

Polynikes, you will find it surprising
and surely shameful
to discover that I prefer your uncouth beard and scarred chin
to the appled cheeks and sheep-soft curls of Diodorus
(that pearl of the *polis*, beloved by girls and philosophers alike).

Yes, it is true that everyone who matters in Athens
says that when Diodorus takes the lyre in his hands
lambent and textured as Parian marble
and holds it to that bouquet of oleander
which is his heart
he is the very sound and picture of Phoebus,
that *kouros* of heaven,
beknighted by tradition as patron and object
of thigh-lusters such as us.

Yet it is also true that, when in danger
of losing a musical contest to rough-skinned Marsyas,
bearded goat-man reeking of grapes and forest,
the manicured deity, ruled by the petty venom
that courses through all edgeless, immortal things,
flayed his opponent alive
and left his hempen skin
a prey to flies.

And was it also not the god of the *kouroi*
who guided the dainty hands
of noble Hektor's shrinking brother,
when they fired the fateful arrow
into the ill-starred heel of that titan-among-men, Achilleus?

Don't tell me I commit sacrilege, friend.
Surely, as a decorated *hoplite* yourself, you can appreciate my position—
if a god (whose very nature necessarily renders him
incapable of courage
in the same way that a mongrel

is incapable of taking wing)
can allow a lion to be slain by a lamb
simply out of spite and favor
then surely it is the gods who are guilty of sacrilege
against all that is holy in men's nature!

These strutting boys and their deep-cutting schemes
may very well be dear to Olympus
(we are told that Ganymede
was a youth of surpassing beauty,
as was Hyacinthus)
but this is only because they mirror
all that is indecent and unmanly in the gods.

And yet, Polynikes, as much as these wanton nymphs put us off
with their violet lips and milk-filled bellies,
we still catch ourselves aching for a tight pair of thighs, don't we?
Round breasts and nectar-sweet moans may please the senses,
but a man, if he is a man,
cannot subsist on the piquancy of figs and raisins.
To my thinking, there's only one solution for those with our tastes.

I anticipate your objections.
How can a man,
who is accustomed to knowing other men
through a lens of metal,
grasp a favorite friend beneath a linen sheet
and afterwards still deal death
and contribute his measure of chaste sweat
to his comrades' enterprise?

A sensible objection, my Peloponnesian friend,
yet you may lay to rest
your qualms of duty and custom.
While it is true that the bronze in your bones,
the fired metal of your irises,
and summer's imprint on your skin all pull me,
as if there were fishhooks in my flesh,
I am drawn not like the groggy bear
who lumbers after the comfort of honey.

Rather, I look upon you as the sun
looks to its apotheosis;
the sun, who, after spending the morning
gazing towards heaven's zenith,

Charlie Bondhus

strives for and settles at the highest point of the firmament,
thus bringing glory to himself
and a colored grandeur surpassing that of a parading phalanx
to the sky that supports him.

Do you think me drunk?
I swear that I have gone nowhere near Agathon's home tonight.
It's in perfect sobriety that I ask

as one who has seen both the breasts of Attic whores
and the nakedness of wounds;
as one who knows why the pulped head of a comrade
shakes a soldier far more
than the broken heart of a wife;
as one who has felt those parts of a man,
secret even to himself,
twist and indent
to accommodate the flint-sharp tip of a *dory*;

what greater love can a man have
than that he holds for the shield bearers
who stand at both of his hands?

Your expression tells me that my words have found
the place where bone touches muscle.
You have much to mull over, *Agapitos*,
but bear with me yet a moment longer
and then if you wish to go, you may.
I will not detain you by the arm or set up camp outside your door
like a blubbering *erastes*, castrated by his own desires.
I have almost said my peace—only this remains:

I offer my arms, sturdier than *dory* or *xiphos*.
My blood will be the cloak you draw about your shoulders,
and my heart is the indispensable *hoplon*
which, in death,
will cradle your body within its scooped basin.

For I think your experience and mine both confirm it, Polynikes—
the man who seeks the nexus of holy tenderness
will find it most readily alongside his fellows
in the split guts of battle,
with all its fire and loosened braids,
with its dirt made muddy with piss,
with its screams and rags, pink holes, yellow bones…

While bloodless sentimentalists might make us barbarians,
those who know
own that when the hearts of men
stand against the red sun,
the shadows they cast
are always broad with armor
and strained with the same longing
that burns nations.

SOME WOULD CALL IT CRUELTY

that liniment poured out on the loosening shoulders—
amber beads that cradle scars not-yet-made, like fetuses in amnion.

But this kind of pain is never perfectly felt,
its force blunted by the wrist-grip of surrender,
strings of chain-linked clematis
kissing into place. Or the thwack of infliction,
thump of sharp and dull, the systole and diastole in which
the heart takes guilty pleasure,
having found so sincere an imitator.

Some call it cruelty, but rather it is the tenderness of beasts
flayed and tanned, skins pummeled and stretched
around the wooden bones of a timbrel.
And when the loud timbrel is sounded we dance (as did
Miriam, with bitter herbs at her heels and milk and honey upon her lips).
We dance to the beater's heavy fingers
and the dulcet skin-sound they create,
and to the saw-toothed jangle that responds,
that cannot help but respond.

D/s LEATHER EMPORIUM

Tired of our bodies,
we have come
to accessorize our nakedness.

Crowding the fluorescent aisles
rubber-eyed cock rings and collars

adorned with the same steely studs
which dot the harnesses

we wear to arrange ourselves
into the shapes that best mimic

lust

which is, after all, an abstraction
and therefore can only be represented
in shapes,
the geometry of cut leather,
two or more bodies fucking,
the physics of a riding crop raised
then brought down.

The submissive too,
the squint of his eyes,
the arch of his back
a waveform of
his moans making
evergreen valleys
between the cold-lashed peaks of rawhide
on a naked back.

LOVE TRIANGLE: PLATO, MY NEIGHBORS, AND ME

Because bodies and their joys
are not to be compared
to drywall installation,
a large and obnoxious party,
or heavy shoes on hard wood,
I will not turn up the volume
on the radio, pound the ceiling with a broom,
throw on my coat
and go out for coffee.

But I also won't
close my eyes
and picture male/male flesh,
the poetry of elbows and knees,
invite myself to one of those transcendent
moments of happy vulnerability.

Instead I'll smile a bit
as I read Plato's old allegory,
where we're all chained in the cavern
of this world,
backs to the wall,
watching shadows cast from above
enact something that's just
really
fucking
cool
on a screen of ragged stone.

Charlie Bondhus

EPITHALAMIUM TO MYSELF AND WALT WHITMAN

As Adam early in the morning,
Walking forth from the bower refresh'd with sleep,
Behold me where I pass, hear my voice, approach,
Touch me, touch the palm of your hand to my body as I pass,
Be not afraid of my body.
                      - Walt Whitman

I found Walt Whitman–

native and slithering in the tall grasses
au naturel save for beard,
true and biological son of Adam and Father Time.

Yet undivorced from the solid world, I
considered averting my eyes and crying:
"Come up from the fields, father!
Show your face
scraped in dead leaves,
smudged with herb juice
and streaming with the sweet, gentle dew
of buttercups."
Thinking book deals and self-promotion I
considered calling
The Daily Sun
The Hanover Press
The New York Times
to report this
cleft of time and space
this bit of transcendental news.
But something about his eyes,
weary yet reckless,
stopped me.
I knew he was ashamed
to go naked about the world, though
clothing only constrained
his meadow meanders.
What wisdom, I thought, could be learned from this
grizzled young gray man?
What childless adventures?
Sensing my hesitation, Walt,
by way of greeting,
spooled his body about my own:

wrinkled ligaments and hairy appendages
encircling my boy-shape,
like Lucifer to Eve
in classical painting.
Grinding white teeth he
hissed affectionately:

To-day I go consort with Nature's darlings, to-night too,
I am for those who believe in loose delights

Bowing then my head
to the priest of nature
unvested save for crabgrass and pinecones
I reverently uttered the responsorial:

For who but you or I understand lovers and all their sorrow and joy?
And who but you and I, dear grandpapa, ought be poets of comrades?

Much to do, needless to say.
Job had to be quit.
Buses had to be boarded.
Messages had to be left
on lovers' answering machines.

I admit I initially judged Walt's value
in terms of brand recognition.
Considering my new companion
a muscle for my rhetoric, I
dragged him on board a Greyhound
and bore him south.

Watching the 6 o'clock news in a D.C. hostel's common room
I learned that we were in no way unique;
Melville was giving a lecture entitled "I am not Ishmael" in Boston, Emerson
was alive and well, already booked to speak at Dartmouth's commencement,
and the Enquirer reported that Isherwood and Auden had gotten a civil union
in Los Angeles.

Appointing himself captain and helmsman
of brotherly mayhem, Walt drew up blueprints
of the White House, shared his plan
to invade the Oval Office
and contrapuntally recite
"The Song of the Broad-Axe"
interpolated with "I Hear America Singing"

to protest outsourcing, encored
by a brideless wedding march.

But, as it turned out, Walt had been
too long in the ground
to remember his own words.
Later that night at the hostel, lying awake
back-to-back in a twin bed, I
heard him singing reimagined refrains
about New York City in his sleep.

Next day on the plane he
pried open my lap-top
with a butter knife he had somehow gotten past security,
found the porn,
and spent the whole flight in the bathroom,
revising every poem in *Calamus*
to assimilate bears and twinks.

Approaching the gray and brown skyline,
noses and beards pointed towards JFK, I
described the violent rise and sudden crash of the towers,
the significance of which he appreciated,
though not the stark irony of 9-1-1.

That night at CBGB's he got in for free
just for having the gumption
to say he was Walt Whitman,
later corroborated
by an NYU adjunct
who happened to be standing near the door.

Wiggling like Mick Jagger
to the rhythm of an all-girl rock band
(called, I think, "The Flaming Cunts")
he danced his hips into my crotch and,
diving from the stage, cried:

I am Walt Whitman! Liberal and lusty as nature!

After the set and two rounds of cosmopolitans,
the moment splintered away as Walt
sustained an unfortunate groin injury
after propositioning the drummer—
a pink-haired girl in zebra halter top.

There was also a moment of jealousy
when my companion fell
fascinated in love
with a leather queen
named Boddi Elektrique.
The divine nimbus of the female form, he proclaimed in amazement,
wedded to the action and power of the male...

Grabbing his freckled arm, I
assured a miffed Ms. Elektrique that
yes his words were complimentary and
yes she could've fooled me.

(Privately got revenge later
by making out with a poet of lesser talent
while Walt was in the bathroom)

Tired of the East Coast and low on provisions we went shopping,
arm-in-arm at a supermarket in California.
Naturally, we ran into Allen Ginsberg and Neal Cassady,
just out of hell and trying to be domestic.
We chatted about their new home in P-Town and
graciously declined an offer of mescaline and a four-way.

At a poetry slam in San Francisco I
introduced him as a cousin to Dodie B.
and later caught him in the bathroom
peeking at Dennis Cooper
on the other side of the divider.

Faced with expository verse,
self-serving metaphor
and the slack-jawed applause of tongue-pierced teenagers
Walt didn't need to be cajoled
into reciting "Whoever You are Holding Me Now in Hand."

The reigning champion, a
heavy girl in black jeans named Rain
(spelled "R-A-Y-N-E")
was surprisingly fine with losing,
dutifully informed me that she'd "SO do" me if I wasn't gay,
thought it was cool that I hung out with Walt Whitman
and asked us if we knew Poe's number.

Bivouacing the next afternoon on Newport Beach,
we witnessed no solemn and slow procession
no halting army
save that of surfer boys, comrades-to-be,
capped in hair gel and highlights (which I patiently explained)
and garbed in soft herbages of chest bristle
that sprang forth from breasts
like joyous leaves.
All the while
a pink umbrella grew
as a lone oak in Louisiana,
behind and above us, as I wondered
what could I, poet who has come,
do to justify his one or two indicative words?

Leaning over, Walt slipped a ring on my finger, then growled:

All lives and deaths, all of the past, present, future,
This vast similitude spans them, and always has spann'd

Overcome by the passionate surreality of it all
I fell back crying:

Dear father graybeard! Lonely old courage teacher!
I ride tonight and every night with you,
spooned in ecstasy
with the evening star on my lips
the thrush warbling in my breast pocket
and lilacs spread across my trembling hand,
inside a wooden box across the open roads of sombre America!

ALLEN F. CLARK

Claim the Sky

ALLEN F. CLARK grew up as an Army brat and lived in England and Pakistan as well as all over the United States. He served as a Navy corpsman in Vietnam. He has lived for the last forty years up and down the West Coast, working in the health sciences. One of his memoir pieces of his service in Vietnam was jury-selected for a live reading in 2011. He has recently reprised the piece in San Diego, where he has lived since 2002. This is the first publication of his poetry.

Allen F. Clark

ELECTION NIGHT
For Matthew, and all the others

Who'd have thought it would come to this,
that night you sat down next to me at the AA meeting,
all cocksure, all falling apart?
Kicked out of your mother's home at 19
by your stepfather:
No room in my house for any faggot!
A few years on the street, getting by
in the usual way brought you to the acid ER light.
The inevitable diagnosis was confirmed:
the virus had been doing its worst
for a good long while.
You came here to this hospice a month ago,
pneumonia-free. Since then, you've lost
the sight in your left eye, begun to have seizures.
There's talk of a brain tumor: tests to come in two days.
You're getting an intravenous toxin to fight
the thrush that's causing the gummy froth between your lips
        and stolen your voice.

It's election night. From every room comes
the chatter of network pundits as
the nation's map lights up with blue and red.
There are a few stalwart grey states—too close to call.
We who are gathered here are hopeful, even confident
that by tomorrow a Democrat will be headed
for the White House, bringing promise
of a new assault on the virus
that's brought us all beneath this roof.
As each state lights up blue,
a broken chorus explodes
like distant fireworks
        from inside each door.

Sean, the wraith who lives across the hall,
knocks on the jamb, comes in
with his perpetual partner: an IV pole.
He's danced what should have been
the final waltz half a dozen times,
but he's still here tonight, nattily decked out
in his Brooks Brothers robe, hair slicked back
        like a matinee idol: the perfect host.

Allen F. Clark

Canapes and...uh...cider... at my place in a little while.
He winks broadly and exits.
You've had a high fever: your bed is soaked.
I ring for David, the aide. He checks your temp,
finds the fever's broken.
Together we bathe you. I logroll you,
hold you close as he changes the sheets.
Clean and cool, you're off over a cliff
        into deep slumber.

I rise and cross the hall to Sean's party.
His ex has brought smoked salmon, *brie en croute*,
pâté, toasts and crackers, grapes and pears.
Three tables are pushed together
and draped with white linen.
All this is anchored by a huge bouquet,
lush and fragrant as the grandiloquence
        of politicians.

As we snack and sip the bubbly, the magic number ticks
across the finish line: the Democrat has won.
Shouts, cheers and whistles erupt all down the floor.
A few dancers even break into the hallway.
It's getting late. I come back, tell you who's won.
You look blank. I ask if you know who's running
for president. You slowly shake your head, reach
for my hand, bring it to your eyes: our signal
you want me to spend the night.
Usually when I do that, it's on the couch.
Tonight you pat the mattress: once, twice, three times—
        Here it will be.

I unload my pockets, lower the bedrail, climb in.
I pull it up and into place again. You smile at me,
reach for my hands, turn yourself
so that we're spooned, my arms around you.
You bring my hand to your lips, kiss it,
put my thumb in your mouth,
fall asleep. I lie awake most of the night,
        listening to the rain.

It's morning, still dark. I rise quietly
as you sleep on,
walk down the hall,
take the elevator,

cross the lobby.
The door wheezes shut behind me.
The rain has stopped, but the wind persists.
Weathered leaves, still holding their tint
of red and gold
blow up around my knees
doing their best to masquerade
        as hope.

TIME EXPOSURE

    Four a.m.
            Lone hustler's
                whistlewhittling
                      on my corner
upwind of loss
        dropping down
                through birdchatter
                      parrotscreech in
                          papaya lust to
dark canyons
        inverted and
                reaching for light
way, way up
        past nimbus,
                even aurora
                      drawn into
                          materiality
in nightsong's
        complex silence
                the miscibility
                      of all sound,
                          a stampede
trying
    to outrun
        sunrise

Allen F. Clark

BULBS
For Earl Bishop

That warm October
  pale bees bumped against
    our window as they hung
      in summer's flowering vine,
  now sere and brown
    in the slanting light.

Inside, we listened to masses
  written for Spanish kings
    and argued about how
      to set out our bulbs beneath
the trio of Douglas firs.

You saw it one way and
  I another. As usual, a few days
    of careful thought brought
the proper balance: species cyclamen,
    fritillaries, tulips and narcissus,
      each marked by its Latin name,
    limned our path through
      many seasons. Then came

the plague, invading our garden,
  every bed and vale. Finally it took you.
I stayed on in that house, watching
  as fewer blooms emerged
    each year, the careful arrangement of color
      broken by empty ground. *That's not
what we agreed upon,* I could hear you say.

Then one spring just a few
  pale trumpets hung toward
    the heavy duff. I burned sage
      to deconsecrate our garden
    and left the firs to stand sentry

as I moved to another town,
  a place where bulbs are bought
    in pots, fully bloomed to yield
      just a week or two of borrowed glory.
That's a cheat! you'd crow.

It's in that place, though,
   that I've found repose, hearing again
      that same Iberian requiem. My dog's
         in my lap as we sit out the sweet last days
      of blueberry season in the lee
    of a dying hurricane,
studying clouds.

I FELL AWAKE

   I fell awake in the middle of the night
      because I had no dream
         to hold me in slumber.
            The Westminster chimes
               whispered and tiptoed back
                  from primal memory, then spun
            from the bedposts to skirl
         round the ceiling and wrap
        themselves among the fan blades.

Their breeze tickled my shoulders
     and my feet began running laps
         beneath the second quilt, tangled at the foot
            of the bed like old men and ancient women,
         who reached with passion barely recalled
      for that dull delirious moon, then dropped
back and away toward morning's cacophony.

Allen F. Clark

GENTIANS

Our tribe has always loved
things of a certain kind of blue,
one that's saturated beyond
the laws of physics
    and nearly past the eye's ability
to see.
We've sought after these objects
everywhere, and they're always
the most cherished things
    in any home. It's recorded that

no matter where
    the Macedonians encamped,
Hephaestion always first unpacked
the goblets of that hue,
    blown for him by the
oracle at the Empyrean source.
The rivers by those camps, it's said,
whether glacier-fed and green
    cascading from the mountains
or webbing broad and brown
    across a desert,
always borrowed color
from that glass. Alexander would have preferred
    practical bronze, but
his lover would not hear of it:
Lovely, breakable things are given us in trust, he said.

And so it was down the many centuries.
Cobalt blazoned our homes,
    every lintel, table and window.
Then, some thirty years ago,
fire from a much darker source,
    and of a color never seen, came forth
to girdle the entire world.
It found us whether serried in
    the finest towns or
hidden on the smallest farm.
As we died, some of our survivors
    melted the treasured glass into memorial panes.

Allen F. Clark

Finally, as our empty homes were themselves
consumed, the molten glass seeped
deep into the earth to lie
sequestered by the ash.

Thus that color lay
  unseen for many years.
This afternoon two boys have found
    their way to a mountain stream that runs
      through a deep space spared
by the hottest flames.
From that streambed rises
  an ash meadow, woven through
    like a divine carpet with flowers
of that prized and ancient blue.
They hang their cups
  as if to shame the sky.

They are so in love, these boys.
One is dark, the other fair.
What are these? The fair one asks.
I don't know, but they're beautiful, his lover replies.
  Is there seed to collect?
It's in this place that the boys rest:
  It's here that they make love.
The flowers look on
and raise their cups
as if to claim the sky.

ORISONS

In Lahore, I rode
my bicycle through
a cloud of red dust to

Mass in a tiny church
where lizards scaled
the stucco walls

and often found their
prayers against gravity
were not enough.

There, an old priest
called out to summon
the line of brown boys

and girls, dressed in blue
and white. He wore a rough
white cotton cassock.

No gaudy vestments for him:
other old men in Rome
wouldn't afford him silk

or even milk for
the children's lunch.
A rupee a week

from my allowance put
a shallow splash into
each child's cup.

Across and down
the road another
old man cried out

from his minaret
through the blowing dust
to call other children

to prayer. No silk
was requested, only milk
and salvation. But no help

came from Mecca, either:
just more promises borne
on the barren sanguine dust.

ARRIVAL

The journey's been
a long and blistering one.
At last I've arrived to find
some rest at this bar/café/fish shack
perched on the meridian
between time and chaos.

I help my old friend Aurelio close.
I bolt the door and roll up
the slatted blinds to watch
the sun's flattened orb
steal the gold from the ocean
as the waves add their protest
to the world's vast music.

Aurelio dries his hands
and lights a lantern.
Together we sit and wait
for the moon to rise and refill
the sea with her silver
as we toss dice and gentle jokes
against the edge of evening.

SUCH A DAY

Such a day, do you remember?
We didn't plan a single minute
beyond a picnic in the hills
above the town.

We found that perfect spot,
looking down at the tile roofs
and on below to the sea.
There was no sound but the breeze
soughing through the neglected
olive orchard around us.
We ate our meal: A loaf of bread,
some sausage and cheese.
A bottle of wine,
a box of figs.
Then we made love.

Afterward,
I couldn't help myself: I stood
to tear from the tree
a wreath to wrap
through your blond curls.
As I turned to place it
I saw our audience:
An ancient bull, ear-torn survivor
of many *corridas* in the city,
stood with his enormous horns,
his huge eyes watching us
through a hand-hewn fence.

We laughed at him, a picture
from our childhood book,
right down to the cork tree
he browsed beneath. He flicked
his languid tail and bent to nibble
the wild daisies around his feet.

We gathered our things
and set out through
the hazy heat,
Cross-cutting the fields
to the unpaved road and north
around the town toward the *playa*.

Allen F. Clark

There we did what boys will do:
a hundred yards of cartwheels
along the wet sand, to collapse
in a tangle of limbs and laughter.
Then we rose to sprint
into the welcoming waves
and swam out
another hundred yards,
then worked back and forth,
in and out to catch each one
as it built and gathered
to carry us back to shore.

Tired at last, we fell again to the sand
And caught our breath. Then we rose
to walk to the fish shack where
the sun-browned *patron*
with the gap-toothed smile
roasted for us his freshest catch,
served on plates of newspaper.

At the stall next door,
we surveyed the tarts offered
by the Danish woman,
her reddened face crowned
by a coil of wheaten braids.
Which one? I asked. You pointed.
The plum and berry it is, I told her.
Something for our evening meal.
She smiled and boxed it up.

We set off across the sand,
up onto the road, into the town.
Its whitewashed houses tilted
across the ever-narrowing streets
over steps worn smooth by
a thousand years of feet.

Over steps placed there
just for us
to take us back to our room
on that perfect day.

Such a day! Ah, me...
Was there *ever* such a day?

Allen F. Clark

COTINIS MUTABILIS

There he was, right at my toe
on our walk this morning, Thanksgiving:
Cotinis mutabilis, the fig-eater beetle.
His back is a deep dull green,
edged in café au lait.
Alive, he was as good as his name,
scarring the fruit on my tree.
Now he's November-killed,
caught in a drift of brown leaves,
palm litter, the cellophane top
of a pack of cigarettes.

He was the terror of café tables
and summer barbecues
with his loud buzzing,
dive-bombing to impress
any nearby mate.
He was swatted at with a shriek—
could so easily have been stomped.
The world's afraid of beauty
it doesn't understand.

This morning I carry him upstairs,
place him on his back atop
a rustic catafalque
on my kitchen windowsill:
a chip of driftwood beside a trio
of persimmons.
His underside is luminous, iridescent.
The three pairs of legs
are intricate, elegant in their
armored and clawed utility.
Their tips are lifted, barely locked,
forever frozen
in praise.

Allen F. Clark

TOMORROW'S MAN

I am drowsy
on the overheated bus
heading home from school
after freshman debate club
has run late,

so late that I've missed
the last direct bus and must catch
another route from the downtown
station. I step out into
the cold, damp air:
diesel fumes and rain,
hissing brakes and valves.

I am walking
through the heavy wooden doors
with their rubber edges
into the waiting room.
Smells of sweet/sour ancient floor wax
and stale cigarettes.

I am moving
toward the warmth of the snack bar and
magazine stand:
Slick, colorful copies of *Hot Rod,*
Argosy, Field & Stream.

I am looking at
another section:
Covers of buxom women,
smiling, coy. They're all very pretty, but

I am confused
that I'm not drawn to them
but stop instead in front
of the single spinning rack
of smaller magazines:
titles like *Physique Pictorial, Demi-Gods* and
Tomorrow's Man.

I see that inside the covers, they're all filled
with handsome men, wearing nothing
but a posing strap, that tiny triangle
of cloth and a piece of string.
Their muscular bodies are oiled,
their pompadours likewise oiled
or their flattops waxed stiff
above their friendly smiles.
Some are Indian chiefs,
others gods or warriors
from some ancient world.
Some look just like the older boys
at school.

I am afraid
that the man behind the counter
will notice the rise in my tight chinos
and yell at me. I step deeper behind
the rack to turn the pages only to hear
my bus called. I replace *Tomorrow's Man*,
hold my books in front of me
hurry past the counter and outside
to jump onto the bus for home.

I know I'm in trouble for being late.
I walk in the door and see that I am deep in trouble.
There sits my mother, one of her Kents
spiraling smoke like an evil wand,
a martini at her fingertips.

I am afraid the shaker on the counter
behind her is not her first.
You're late. Dinner's in the oven. Go and call your sister.
The three of us eat in silence. My sister
goes upstairs to her homework. It's my turn
to clear the table. She lights another Kent,
watches me. *What's the trouble, son?*
You're very quiet tonight.

I reply that things aren't going well
in debate club, we're all stuck. I'm tired.
No, it's more than that, she says.
*You're really not yourself. It's not good
to bottle things up. Tell me
what's wrong.*

I decline, mumble about homework
as I leave the kitchen, head upstairs,
into the den, turn on the blond wood TV.
I lie down on the rough brown tweed daybed,
try to watch the screen. The show is
'I've Got a Secret.'

I find, though, that my mind begins
instead to turn the pages of those magazines.
My fingers loosen my zipper and then
the waist of my chinos, pull myself out.
It's the blond with the crewcut and
the confident smile. No, it's the brunet
with the surly pout and huge thighs.
Soon it no longer matters which one
he is as the pages turn. One after the other
I gaze at them as my hand
moves faster.

I hear the door open and I smell smoke
and then she speaks: *Well, excuse me,*
backs out and shuts the door.
I veer back, struggle to recapture the moment,
in the form of the man with tight wavy hair
it would be red
and dense freckles and the posing strap
it would be bright blue to match his eyes
bulging below his narrow waist
and above his bulging thighs and yes,
he is mine, I am his, and yes...
I am
        Tomorrow's Man.

NICK COMILLA

THE END OF PRETTY

NICK COMILLA was born on a military base turned ghost town in Rome, New York, and grew up in rural Pennsylvania. He has spent the last five years in Montreal. He graduated from the Creative Writing program at Concordia University and is now working on his MFA in poetry and fiction at The New School in New York City. He was a finalist for the 2011 Irving Layton Poetry Prize for his poem "Pure Form." Previous publications include the September 2012 issue of *Poetry Is Dead* magazine. His short fiction is forthcoming in *Jonathan* (Sibling Rivalry Press).

LINES

In the month of September
I pay for the sins of the summer
as the doctor stitched the needle
through my gashed knuckle gushing
blood I thought about love while I cussed
fuck. Stuck under the thundering sound
of belts unbuckling*, a boy becoming something.
But only pressed together quickly forever leaving
veins pumping language fiendlike and needing
a new way for these veins to be beautiful, bleeding.

In September I'm seeking distraction from distractions,
every line break I see contains nothing but slashes
I find them intriguing /
like gashes in knuckles /
or the way tongues slit /
our words, oral sluts /
when we overuse lines /
and say too much. /

Underneath icicle eyes lay lines, a narrative.
Others lied before me. Pierce & penetrate his skin.
Lines & slashes line our bodies. Proof of living.
Lines are merely slashes that have collapsed
in on themselves. Lines are actors. Like I love you.
You wrap me in white linen, show me lines can lie
down honestly too. Woven down the mattress, they slash us.
(Hush.) (Your lines parenthetically bend, and hold me tightly.)

Yet our lips always start to slash 'em again.
These lines in the subtext of an SMS. The way we read sex
into every lying line. Lines never let dead dogs lie

next to me in this bed. Linen weaves webs in my head.
Those cheekbones as sharp as diamonds. Cold words
(never enough) slash at me like splashing slush.
The sky bright black. This fistful of flesh, the lull of lust.
I want snow like violence. Freeze us while we slowdance.

---

*"under the sounds of belt unbuckling" is a line from "Maelstrom" by C. Dale Young which has been loosely adapted into this poem.

Nick Comilla

Let the wind whip my face like those unbuckled belts.
Note how the snowflakes taste: a little like someone else.

Slashes are more becoming of exes.
What is an X but two slashes crucified, annexed?
Us two slashes caught without an exit. Sentir, sortir.
Always one last time, be my accented é, indicate
past tense. Yet we're infinitive. Present intense, ecstatic.
And when we're absent? No nous is good nous.
But after a break the lines return. No muse is bad muse.

Line breaks suggest that something next is about to come
even when it never does. We're always only about to come.
Because we're always chasing the same person
dressed up in different clothes / masquerading perfect.
That's why love is a drag: a Queen we worship.
Much like men, she comes and then she goes.
As transient as gender / as radiant as never / never /
land where you'll find Peter Pan / all the lost boys holding hands /
forever floating
but never really flying /
forever trying
to be Superman.

O Captain! My Captain! / oh my Whore, my hero /
with zero masks in your muscular masculinity /
the definitive Divinity of the end of pretty /

little springtime things with flowers in their hair... Meet me up in the air
where I'm always dreaming / eighteen through twenty now twenty three me—
somewhere in between you & me there's a piece of you I'm seeking
permit me to keep it if you won't keep me.

While you're as scared as ever of being discovered by another,
I think about your father. Raise me like the sun to the symbol of the razor
that he gave you on your 31st birthday. Show me the way if you know.
Or retreat under the covers. You offer me more couverture.
How smooth you are, completely / incomplete like me.

Your young face despite your age. The sexiness of on and off interest.
A man-boy with a mortgage. The fleeting meaning in your language.
The French in between your whimpers. My soft hands hard against yours.
As I whisper: I / fucking love / fucking you /
when I really meant to say I fucking love you.

But you won't teach me how to shave my face,
how to slash my mask to be your boy.
Or how to be your man, non plus,
as I run amok up inside your guts
you can't show me because you're still learning, handsome thing.

Forever rejecting and never promising
the only ring around me, this pink prince of conquest,
his ominous prick of dominance.
Our little deaths our boyishness,
il fait l'amour pour resister a la mort.

Wrap me in linen, then in plastic.
(Cover me, comfort me). I won't
be unrealistic: past ghosts
and concurrent angels fall
for your lines too. I won't
pretend if I can't make believe.

Every night you let me in, make me
feel like a man. A beautiful repeating
one night stand. When it ends,
will you still be a lost boy?
A never-never man?

*

Trente-deux ans. De plus en plus seul a chaque année.
As your hair gets thin like the boys you like,
watch it fade from dirty blond to shades
of Dorian Gray. You drain the soul of youths
to use them. Your beauty, our burden.
But no painter drew you, lover. He'll draw the shades.
Your slashing words lie line after line.
Et c'est comme ça, homme-garçon
que, bientôt, tu vas rester la-bas,
avec tes lignes, en chaîne. Seul. Et laid.

CAMP FIRE

We are allowed no other lovers. Merely fucks: fuckers.
One timers. Non-over nighters. It's dangerous to refrain.

Because the way people smell gets tattooed on the brain.
Life is like poetry: built around constraint, through refrain.

We know the value of the couplet. The discipline it takes
to expand out, briefly tercet, fuck 2nd person: *You*. (Refrain.)

Step away. This can never happen again. I cannot complain.
It's just a onetime thing. Anything more would be a taboo refrain.

"Why?" *You* whines, begging, asking the same questions again and
again. Because *We* are blood brothers. No redo through refrain.

Because the man I'm with falls on me like rain*. *You* smells new, unique—
of camp fires. *You* will be stomped out. Our rain doesn't stop for a new refrain.

"The couplet is oppressive." It's hard to abstain. "Can't we just villanelle,
run around, then come back again?" *You* wants an occasional, smooth refrain.

You says I use people. So many you's being used. I throw them out
like used condoms. *You* says screw you, fuck you, fine, please do refrain.

Screw me, fuck me, ask nothing else of me. Now *You* get it, exactly!
The truth is, *You*, I'm almost twenty-two. I know when not to refrain.

---

*"fall on me like rain" is a line adapted from "Maelstrom" by C. Dale Young

MONTREAL SESTINA

I can't believe you started fights over places like Unity.
I wasn't allowed to go with you, "*period!*" Parking
was out of the question too. Neither of us liked Sky
and one time it was over that sketchy bar (...ew) Taboo,
referring to underage boys. No money for cover—and the bar Stud
wasn't of interest either. All these names make no sense: Oasis.

Why call a bath on St. Cath "Oasis"?
Right across the street that other lie: Unity.
As if a sauna could offer refuge from aberzombie studs
whose bodies clog the streets like bad cars, bad parking.
Here's some truth. Dancing at clubs or in bars like Taboo
you'll see everyone, except the person in front of you. The sky

isn't black enough for all these shooting stars. That summer at Sky
your shimmer dimmed quickly, stumbling drunk alone to Oasis.
Sucking the dick of some lonely vieux monsieur for cash. Taboo
to mention that pederast, eh? You candyass. Couldn't kiss me after, unity
we created, or faked it, pissed away at places like Parking—parking
everywhere except at the drive in. Imaginary: you whispering hush, stud,

as I ponder life's leather complexities, fucking so hard tire studs
imprint the earth, my chest pressed against yours like how the sky
presses star signs down onto us. Reality: non-monogamy, ie, Parking,
Sagittarius sans Gemini, your fickle heart merely a man's oasis.
A place briefly lit, a cigarette, the way you suck it and stub unity,
stripping off love quicker than the clothing of nouveaux-danseurs-nues à Taboo.

It was shocking at first. Slicing you off of me, too, like a bad tattoo,
withdrawal from you was worse than stupid stuff we do: acid, poppers, studs
if we've drunk too much, sex over love, designer drugs and that false unity
flooding my brain in serotonin waves. Cigarettes like telescopes, the sky
revealing a thousand plastic wax bitch Icaruses. I want a real oasis,
to dance from star to star avec un autre Rimbaud, passing over Parking

and hardly caring! I'll wake up in sunlight someday. You? Still at Parking,
flirting, searching, lying beautifully in two languages, feeling blue, taboo
just to hold his hand for longer than a minute. You'll get older then, at Oasis,
neon blond hair thinning early. Your hands clean from never holding, an STD,
however, is a very real possibility. In Montreal boys fade out faster than the sky
turns black, turning on the night life. As for that club, burned down twice? Unity

is still standing, bass thumping, Parking too. Another young stud
tastes the taboo things this city offers, entering a sandcastle Sky
no longer lonely as an oasis. Brief feelings. Fast flickering lights. Unity.

BAD BOY'S SLUT SONG
After "Sad Boy's Sad Boy" by Charles Bernstein
& "Mad Girl's Love Song" by Sylvia Plath

We romp the bed and all the sheets slide bad
I trick my treats and all is sweet again
I slut I fuck you up inside our lust

The trains go zooming out in blue and white
And boys in bloom glide in
We ride the tracks while all the ice sleets bad

Electro thumps our heads too much
And jumps me out tonight bright black
I handcuff I fuck you up inside our lust

I lube my stroke and all the dudes glide glad
I trick my treats and all is kink S/M
I stub my smoke and the skin sizzles sad

I shift your shaft the way you said
But I lose myself in roles we play
We hop in bed and all the sheets drift jazz

At last when fuck stops it all comes back again
A ruin my sheets and all the boys bloom bad
I slut I fuck you up inside our lust

PURE FORM

The problem with sex is that it makes me stupid.
No one *really* talks about Sartre or Camus naked.

And if they do, they're probably faking it.
That sound of pretense when they're—oooh—naked.

The problem with sex is... well, Foucault. He ruined it.
Social construction is not of much use, naked.

Except this: how many people do we go with just to make it?
A boy from Du Bois (pronounced Do Boys) that moaned "dude" naked.

First of all, I told him, it's French. It's pronounced *Do-Bwah*.
It means "some woods." Some Americans make me say "ew," naked.

Accept this. Oppression is pervasive. Sexual revolution has been academized.
And calculated, compromised. Now the goal is marriage: sexual déjà vu, naked.

And yet I can't help but feel that clothing is a cage. Our only solution
to our sweatshop tattoos is to be totally unglued. Naked.

I just wish we could do it gracefully. So many things get in the way.
Have you been tested? The awkward shuffle for a condom and lube, naked.

Promiscuity is Russian roulette. I don't want to be bound to anyone,
the problem with "a couple" is that it's only two. But can we be too naked?

Stripped to fakeness? As if I want to be nineteen again. Waking up next to a man,
the taste of beer still on my tongue, *where am I? who the fuck are you?* Naked.

I still want to be an animal, yet with a more pure form. If the body is art,
naked suggests negation. I want to be complete. Completely nude, naked.

SHADOW HIM

The first time I met him,
in the back, by the fountain,
mouth wrapped 'round that faucet,
the maze of white tile and old shower
rooms, abandoned, just us—until

the quick squeak of sneakers,
the scuff marks, the mesh shorts
danced me dizzy on the basketball
courts. Practice spent pretending
we weren't staring. The ball spinning
around his middle finger like the sun.

Just hoped that coach didn't notice
that us two players were really on
the same team, there was really no
need back then to exchange numbers,
already conveniently slapped on our backs.

After weeks of practice we white lie
to coach and parents. We say
we stay after, getting a ride with
so and so, whoever. Now the scoreboard
don't keep score. The whole court
to ourselves, running up and down
each other, the sweet swish
of breath and nets together.

The sun on his fingertips went down
as the sky-high windows turns us into
silhouettes. He taught me his tricks—
how to palm a ball,
how to dribble between his legs,
and then he told me to shadow him,
and stick to him, behind him,
with my entire body I shadowed him.

Nick Comilla

UNDERNEATH THE SURFACE

I stare at him through the glass
on the bleachers during gym class.
At fifteen. I wish I was the ice.

Can imagine him skating all over me
piercing, yes, a blade yes, cruising
up and down my body, scarring,
splitting me open maybe,
spinning figure eights on me,
slapping his stick on me,
oh player please fall on me.

Running out the time on me,
skating backwards on me,
holding the hand of your first
girlfriend on me. Turning
me to slush, me melting. Stabbing
your blade into me, look
one foot only on me, going
the fastest on me, spilling
a cherry slush puppy on me.

On your hands and knees on me.
Falling hard on your ass on me.
Going around in circles with me.
No padding, no protection,
just you and this violent dance
swirling around on me.

If I were the ice I'd be outside
of the rink. Can imagine a lake
of feeling beneath me, begging me
to break open and greet you
splashing. Doggy paddle failing.

Suddenly it happens,
me cracking. You falling on me,
falling into me. Swallowed up in me
slipping under me quickly,
being weighed down by
the pure icy weight of me.
Arms flailing, never let go of me.

Nick Comilla

All your friends gliding, panicky,
how could this happen? You were
always so graceful with me.
I pull you down drowning
in me, please just love me.

BACK IN THE NINETIES

Back in the nineties
you would push me
up against the wall
in the locker room.

You would push in
and tell me to stay. "Please,"
echoing in the locker room,
my body bent, a slight slant.

Telling me to say please, my
swim trunks 'round my knees,
your body in me. Slight slants
making waves with my hips

as other boys splash and swim.
On my hands and knees, together
we made waves with hips, and yet
you would never press our lips

together. Swimming in your hands
I remember how you taught me
tricks that forever impress—I'll never
forget how to back flip off the high dive.

I remember how you told me
my eyes were more blue than water as
you flipped me on my back, diving
in, even then, you weren't gentle.

My eyes more blue than any water
trickling down. Up against the wall
pressed against me. You weren't gentle
back in the nineties. You were nineteen.

JIM CORY

Opus 121

JIM CORY, in addition to all kinds of writing, takes an interest in reptiles, birds, history, painting, the piano, architecture, yoga and strange conversations overheard. Not necessarily in that order. Poems have appeared recently in *Apiary, Burp, Court Green, Lungfull!*, and *Skidrow Penthouse*. He has been the recipient of fellowships from the Pennsylvania Arts Council and Yaddo and was, in 2000, the first winner of the Richard Hall Memorial Short Story Award, given by the Lambda Literary Foundation. Rain Mountain Press published *No Brainer Variations* in 2011. He lives in Philadelphia.

Jim Cory

OPUS 121

Hearing aid card arrives
out of the blue. (Orange,

actually.) **CALL US TODAY**. How do
they know? *We strive*

    to offer you
    the best instruments
    available. As if this

were a message from the dildo
factory. And if I dipt my shoe

in dog-doo
would you smell it?
                     A stranger
                     to Brian R.'s sister

on the El: *I hope ya*
step in shit the resta yer life! Doors

close. *Whush*. Oh, the senses
tender their resignation

in increments. Tho not always.
Jerry C. used to marvel at the way

his olfactory faculty
packed a bag & ran away

overnight. *Couldn't smell*
    a goddamned thing. Described
        in the same tone

w/which he bragged
    about all the
        men he'd bed

ded after divorcing his wife
    at 49. *I had more sex*
        than I'd ever had

in my life. His ex-
    & he still friends. A miracle. I remember

Jim Cory

        poking my nose in a bowl

of hyacinth wonder'd
what it'd be like if it all came

            back
            blank.

Absent their odor do flowers
exist? Or become

color & texture, another
anything? I'll know when

I get there. Weird tho
when the ears wear out.

> *We know how*
> *your noise has*
> *undergone invisible,*
> *digital and fully*
> *programmable tech*
> *nology breakthroughs*

Oh, do you? Are you aware that someone
speaking w/o diction

sounds like a wounded tape recorder

staggering thru the Tunnel of Love? Occasional flash

        of actual pitch.
     (Kisses) Consonants
          tiptoe thru cracks.

    The rhythm of the sentence

        hangs suspended
for an instant. As in
      the flight path
that starling just took.

And where words were

        vowels expand

to fill in the blanks while the mind

        supplies all sorts of

interesting bullshit. *Merry Christmas, delicious.*

            (Why would Billy
            say something like
            that? And in July?)

Hearing's merely convenience
like the rest of it

        but when limit

ed to frequencies in single digits

           charges the usual banalties
           w/vim. Fun, sometimes

tho a pianist pounding
soundlessly across keys would send

a strong signal
        that one's days

as a regular in concert halls
had about ended. Major drag. Faure,

           deaf as a board
           sat on the boards

of a Sorbonne stage, 1922, while an orchestra performed
a sampling of his *oeuvre* in national homage. Observers note

           the way his face
                —"gazing pensively"—
           occasionally
                took a stroll.

Revisiting the nest from which his notes
rose on luscious mustache wings. Canned

from his post as director
of the **Conservatoire**, the maestro languished

til taking up the string quartet heard

by me now but (by Faure) only in his head.

Opus 121. His last.
Things in motion vibrate

a number of times called frequencies
& land as tunes (unless dammed by ear wax)

        along some portion of the primary
        auditory cortex. And where

        exactly, is air
        in all this? A question posed by

        the opening movement's
        5-note figure on viola.

        On one of our outings Richard S.
        whispers something about

        what "the violins"

        are up to.

        "Those're
        violas,"

        I hiss & watch that face
        unmake itself

        like a bed
        remembering bad

        sex. Regretted

it later. Would he have regretted
being here to experience

such absurdities as
Bush 2, or the Macarena?

        Half the joy of the world
        's top-selling hearing aid
        is hearing companions
        clearly, comfortably, and...

            & who

Jim Cory

    needs to

    when they blab
    on endlessly

    about them
    selves

Meanwhile imagine
life w/o reading glasses. Or

losing 2 pair in a day. Which
raises the question: which goes 1st

        or fast
        er: the ability to gather data

or the means
to ascertain what it means?

        Centipedes traipse by in migrating
        lines of blur. Have to get what Jack calls

"Old Queen Strings" those drugstore straps
for specs to dangle on. So gay.

And if I can't see
that well, what do people see

when they see

        me? (A look
        from that hottie at the gym, as in: Who let

it out?) We all reach a point where
nothing we wear

        enhances the sensual appeal. Probably.
        Did you ever get laid

in Lima, Ohio? I
did. Just kidding. Tried

once in Saginaw but that must be why
they call it that. Droops. Successful

        in Nashville

tho so

hungover I said *good morning* to
the manikin my host

had posted for a joke at the kitchen table. He laughed
& lit a cigarette. *Honey, you need a Bloody.*

        Ouch.
        Touch.

JIM CORY
OR CURRENT OCCUPANT

    ...these amazing technologies
    experience noise companions
    breakthrough undergone

Peer past tangerines at that Chinese

guy in the Reading Terminal Market. Jeff. Excellent
English tho we have no need

        for language as such
        on that particular afternoon.

Shows me his cache of erotic prints
stashed in the closet w/the Heisey glass. Some queen

he'd met pointed him toward collecting. Genetic candelabra
w/crystalline tears attached. My dears! They blow'em

in Newark, OH, honestly, where a bank by Louis
Sullivan (bitchy, brilliant, bow tie) was built & still stands

an abandoned ice cream parlor. Recall'd w/all
the joy de vivre of that romp w/Michael S.

in the room he rented on Allen St. in State College.
House no longer there. The closecropt hair on his

    small round
    head smells like

    crotch perfume & makes me

    so much want to fuck

>   his small round

>   ass. Rainy

afternoon, that one, pass'd like a squall. Became
a nurse. Calls years later

at noon, high on morphine, wanting to know
how & why I stopt drinking. Disappears

in the plague. To think about sex
every (waking) hour & then not at all

like changing trains for the coast
in Chicago. Get on the Southwest Chief

& there's the vaguest odor
of all those people

staring into all that land
for all those miles.

>   Smell
>   foretells

everything. *Even in the noisiest environments.* "Don't look now but
that mothball at the bar

just sent you a drink." More than once
I rewarded their generosity w/ *programmable* rudeness. Piaf

>   famously had no regrets
>   but that was stage bravado. At 25

50 is inconceivable. At 60
you've lived thru 30

>   twice.
>   Imagination

requires higher voltage.
Hepburn in her dotage

>   reportedly ordered the mirrors throughout her house
>   removed. *Jamie, why are you*

staring at me like that?

Jim Cory

Is my hair coming down?

        Had assistants do
        her do

& make-up. I hope she wasn't
partial to spinach. Worse than forgetting

to zip one's fly. Jesus, the things
we see. Saw

a drunk proceed down Broad Street once
at 11 AM w/his dick

hanging out the slit of grass-stained khakis.
Office worker Shock & Awe.

The dangling dingus undid them. Face
of its owner fix'd in bewil

dered dignity, as if
it took everything he had

to avoid
knocking a buil

ding over.

CARLTON FISHER

Carrion in Waiting

CARLTON FISHER is a doctoral student at SUNY Binghamton and an English Instructor at a small liberal arts school in New York, near the Canadian border. He grew up on a small family farm, and much of his poetry deals with the loss of his mother at age 16 and the effects it had on his family. He is the author of the self-published chapbook *Silhouette of a Man*. He spends his spare time with his dog, Gilbert, and various cats, attempting to renovate his house within the confines of his limited architectural ability.

www.facebook.com/carlton.fisher3

JANUARY 2012: EXODUS

They call it hazing—
the small explosions,
like gunshots,
that turn the sky black and shrill
with caws of protest.

For a week,
the crows cover the trees of my neighborhood
like giant black leaf buds,
skeletons of winter trees covered in murders,
noisy with their conversations.

The echoes of the sharp reports
chase them from the square to the park
and back again,
the somber tenants of our city
refusing to vacate their stations.

The officials say
it is the heat of the buildings
that draws them in winter,
neglecting to explain
the clouds of them that fly above Public Square
in July and August.

They are the eternal shadow of this city,
the reminder
we are all carrion in waiting.

ROMANCE NOVELS

My mother always woke up
hours before she needed to,
because my father was a slow riser,
and she had to speak to him repeatedly
to get him to wake up to milk the cows,

unless she did it alone.

She sat under the yellowed light in our kitchen
reading romance novels at two in the morning,
drinking her coffee,
going into the bedroom every ten minutes,
saying, "David, it's time to get up."
My father would roll over,
say in his sleep, "C'mon, let's go,
gotta get up, c'mon,
we need to get going."

As though he was the one waiting.

She would go back to her coffee—
his living snooze alarm—
working her way through
Danielle Steele, Victoria Holt, Erica Jong.
If she were alive now,
I imagine she would be an acolyte
of Nicholas Sparks, Nora Roberts,
and bodice rippers
where women with heaving bosoms
barely contained by their too-tight corsets
sought solace in the embrace
of a half-naked man
at the base of a waterfall
or in front of a field of wild horses.

My mother slept at the very edge of their bed,
precariously balanced on the verge of tipping into oblivion—
the farthest point she could get from my father
without sleeping in another room.

She told me once that she married him
only because she thought no one else would ask,

first considered divorce
the week they returned from their honeymoon.

I still see her at that table,
reading romance novels,
trying to find the heat of passion
in the winter of her marriage.

WITHOUT

I woke up at sunrise,
your body breathing beside me in the bed.
The sound of the birds singing outside
was almost deafening.

I moved quietly to go to the bathroom,
not wanting to wake you.
As I stepped into the hall and shut the door,
I realized all I could hear anymore
was the rain falling.

It seemed appropriate.

THE BAD HOUSE CLEANER'S CONFESSION

Your boxers are still lying on the floor
just beneath the edge of the bed skirt.
I pretend to not notice they are there,
thinking maybe if they lay there long enough,
you'll eventually come back to find them.

SCARIFICATION

Despite stereotypes,
if they sit together long enough,
even gay men will discuss their scars.
In a show and tell of injury,
we'll pull up our shirt sleeves,
roll up pant legs,
point to memories that have left their marks.

I can list mine easily:
here is the one from falling in the driveway
when I was two
and getting a pebble stuck in my head
(the scar, by the way, the doctor assured my parents
would disappear in six months or less);
here is where I fell off my bike
while trying to get into shape;
here is where I took extreme measures
getting rid of a pimple
and left a permanent mark
that looks like a pimple;
here is where my grandmother's cat
taught me about keeping my distance.

(I don't show the hernia scar
unless we've had too much to drink
or I am looking for an excuse
to undo my pants.)

My friends have scars less frivolous.

"This is the scar
where the soldier dragged me out of the barracks
by my hair and tore my scalp
when he found out his roommate and I
were more than just friends."

"This is where my father hit me
with the rock
when I told him I was gay."

"This line is where he cut me
when I told him that I loved him

and he called me a fag."

We show the scars
that illustrate our histories,
but we don't talk about the ones inside—
the ones that are invisible
unless you get close enough;
then you can even see those too.

CLEANING THE PAINT ROLLERS

A friend tells me
it's not customary
to rinse the paint from the roller,
reuse it for the next project,
that they are meant to be thrown away.

And I remember hours in childhood,
scrubbing rollers under the pressure
of the garden hose—
thick rivulets of paint
running down the driveway,
forming colored puddles at the base of the hill in the dirt.

It would be so much easier now
to clean them—
the plastic tube at the center
would not crush and pulp
like the cardboard core in the old rollers,
would not ruin the entire thing,
make it unusable,
make it a waste.

I have spent over 30 years of my life scrubbing rollers
just because I thought that's what was done.

It's amazing how easy it is
to become used to poverty,
accustomed to lack,
to need without knowing
that you need at all.

PERSISTENCE

Salvador Dali is alive and well
and sitting in a jail cell
after raving in a watch shop
that no one understands him.
The time he sits there
runs down the walls in drips and drizzles
and pools on the floor in puddles
of minutes that mix with hours
until they are mopped up with towels
that reek of lost years.

"Memory and memory and memory,"
he chants,
dipping his fingers into pools
and tracing the outlines of what he remembers
of his after life
on the cell walls.
"It slips like water
through a filter,
and all I'm left with
is the sediment of years,
the silt from the bottom of the well."
His heart breaks at the digital numbers
of the clock high on the wall.

At midnight,
he spits through the bars of the cell,
tells the guard that was the first year of the revolution,
scrawls "I am not watched;
I am the watcher,"
on the walls with his bloodied fingertips,
and in the morning he is gone,
as the sunlight slides across the pools
of time splashed across his floor.

GHOST BROTHER

I remind people of their brothers,
usually their dead ones.
My face is a Rorschach block
onto which people project
the images of what they've lost.

You look just like him
they say.
*You hold your head the way he did,
tell his jokes.*
I am the ghost in the room.

I miss him so much,
they tell me
and buy me a coffee.
You have his eyes.

Sometimes they tell me childhood secrets,
things only their brothers knew,
search my face for some recognition
as though I'd been sent back,
given one last opportunity
to hear their confessions.

I think about my own brother,
a casualty in the war with my parents,
how we have no secrets we share.

How,
with eight years between us,
we were more like strangers than siblings.

In my mind,
he is still eight years old,
wearing Ninja Turtle pajamas
and making sandwiches in the kitchen
when no one was looking.

Ben, I'm sorry I wasn't there,
am not there now,
that I am probably just as much a mystery to you
as you are to me,

that I meet no one that reminds me of you,
and that I would have nothing to talk about with them
if I did.

AVANT GARDE

I dreamt I was an avant garde performance poet.
I told people truths they didn't want to hear
in ways that made them willing to believe.
It was beautiful.

I read
each
word
as though
I had
been trapped
inside
The Matrix,
like
Keanu Reeves,
only with,
you know,
emotion.

I told them
each person
has a secret name
that only their other can know
and when it is spoken
it becomes
your only name.

And I was famous
and powerful
and did not live under a bridge,
which is how I knew it was a dream.

THE POPULAR BOYS AT THE TEN-YEAR REUNION

The popular boys had soccer-strong bodies
that they hid from me in the locker room,
as though I couldn't be controlled.
They had girlfriends on the cheerleading team
who gave them amateur blowjobs,
some of which ended in vomiting
and become the stuff of legend.
They had tight boy-skin stretched over the ripple of muscle,
taut along the jaw lines that supported their sneers
when the faggot walked down the hall,
told jokes about queers,
and made grandiose displays
of covering their asses
as though I would make them the stars
in a reenactment of that scene from *The Accused*.

At the ten-year reunion,
the popular boys had beer guts,
receding hairlines,
and bored housewives
who called them "hon"
with that tone that barely covers homicidal intent

Fuck you, I win.

EDMUND MILLER

SLAPSHOTS À GO GO

EDMUND MILLER has published numerous poetry chapbooks and a book of erotic stories called *Night Times*. His major poetry books are the legendary *Fucking Animals* and the monumental *Go-Go Boy Sonnets: Men of the New York Club Scene*. This last book uses the traditional sonnet sequence to explore the world of the male dancers of gay New York, combining lightness of tone with a seriousness of purpose by relating real-world lives to performance and depicting interaction with patrons to emphasize that there is more to the men than beauty. His current creative work focuses on drama with such plays as *The Greeks Have a Word*, *Royal Favorite or Regime Change*, *The Last Conquests of Beau Fersen*, *Cold Feet*, and *The Colonel's Lady*. The nationally recognized authority on the *Sylvie and Bruno* books of Lewis Carroll, Miller is also author of scholarly books about seventeenth-century British literature, including three about the poet George Herbert.

www.go-goboysonnets.com

SNAPSHOT

Your picture's just fallen to the floor
denting its fake gold frame,
and now the glass is broken,
and I can see you only there
behind the cracks again. Really
I'd forgotten all about it. But
it seems it had been resting
on my desk since you left
whenever it was that that was.
You are smiling in the picture—
that is always a mistake—
ever so forever and ever it seems.
Your smile brings back no memory
nor touches any loss though
your picture is here before me now
underfoot. Yet I think of poor you,
for so well as I can recall
you forgot ever to ask for mine.

NO GORILLA

Then one day you suddenly know
that you're not a gorilla
and there's no use pretending you are
so you slouch in your seat
and you slouch when you stand
and go limp
in your dungarees.

VOYEUR

Creeping to the window
shrouded in the artificial night
of all indoors,
I spy the little boy next door
angling on the sofa
in his underdrawers, there
before him his bated brother,
the bigger boy next door,
equally next to naked,
flailing his arms in exercise
fore and aft and checking
periodically his chest
for the tell-tale swollen
bruises of success.

SPURS

When I look at him
through my black eyes
I see blood on his hands
and melting wax
there in the dark.
There's a metal stud
on his zipper hook.
He wears black leather pants
to bed
and doesn't take his boots off.
And there's a whip on the nighttable
but no lubricants.
Oh it's true there's a scar
on his forehead
where the beltbuckle hit
and blood of his own
in the hair
on his chest.
But by his light
he's all right.
He doesn't fight.
It's just me.

LICENSE PENDING
For Victor Daniel*

While he mixes drinks meticulously,
Victor's thick silver chain musically clanks
Against his even thicker chest and yanks
My chain. I behave ridiculously,
Moon over his five o'clock shadow, sink
Into black pools of eyes that mesmerize.
Star-struck, I imagine his gym-built thighs.
Yet he hands me his number with a wink.

This business card stuns me with a long list:
Professional board certification
In pulmonary resuscitation
And the same certification for tryst
With trainer/astrologer/hypnotist.
License to love's the only one he's missed.

---

*Victor is a board-certified hypnotist (R.H.) and certified personal trainer (A.C.E.). Educated at S.U.N.Y. Stony Brook and also professionally certified in cardiopulmonary resuscitation, he casts horoscopes, models, and sometimes even tends bar—formerly at Uncle Charlie's and at Silver Lining in Floral Park, later at Splash. He saw the 1998 New York City restriction on bare-bottomed bartending (happily no longer enforced) as a violation of his civil liberty. He has a daughter, Destiny, born on Halloween in 1995. He says he sometimes feels like "a lesbian trapped in the body of a man." Donald Charles Richardson interviewed Victor for a photo essay in the August 1999 issue of *Exercise for Men Only*.

Edmund Miller

THE LEGACY OF ISADORA DUNCAN
For Joshua*

Joshua's a Little Ivy Leaguer.
Although his lanky but muscular frame
Is small too, he sports a large claim to fame.
Willing to be ogled—in fact eager—
He's shelved the degree he sought to enhance
With pre-med sequence, and he's suddenly
In film school and at the Joffrey. And he
Studies Martha Graham techniques of dance.

But career vacillation has its share
Of unification: he aims to make
Isadora his idol—though he'll take
The care she failed to not to get neckwear
(Or another dangling appendage)
Caught in some mechanical assemblage.

---

*Joshua is a graduate of Williams College, where he majored in music while completing the pre-medical program. At the time this poem was written, he was a go-go dancer on the New York club scene. At present he is putting most of his energy into studying for a career as an opera singer, so he has left the go-go boy circuit. But he does still work as a personal trainer.

IN THE PORNO THEATER

Now suddenly everyone's hot to be
      Tight with me. Why, I'm all aglow tonight!
      At least I must be doing one thing right
Since sitting rub-a-dub snug beside me
Is a guy who's passed me up many times.
      Yet he lunges for my little nipper,
      Fingering my crotch, oping my zipper,
Hoisting me erect, setting off my chimes.

But all the while this expert boldly sucks,
I long for something worth the whole nine bucks
Paid at the door. At last I catch the eye
Of a better guy, eye-lashed, standing by.
      Groping this hunk enables me to shoot,
      But, then, I find he gives my hand the boot.

THE ORANGE CHALLENGE

For Warren Beatty, in the hot seat during
      Splendor in the Grass *and* The Roman Spring of Mrs. Stone
      and then again during Dick Tracy *and* Truth or Dare

Although Madonna says he never has been manned,
      Once there was near surrender in the grass
      When William Inge flew a protégé first class
Down Puerto Villarta way, performance safely canned,
To introduce Him-of-th'Enormous-Thing
      To Tennessee in his orangery
      Seeking sunkissed liquidy mercen'ry
Rentier to juice up *The Roman Spring*.

Warren's tongue boldly proved Italianate.
Tennessee, feeling he had no need to wait,
Approved him, thinking—at some later date—
He would languidly reciprocate.
      But Warren never came across. No one, bar Inge,
      E'er again in splendor squeezed that orange.

LAP DANCE

Sitting at the bar
With my stool turned to the side
So I can scope the room,
I receive a casual visitor
Who leans across my lap
To place an order.
I run my fingers down his back
Tracking the line
Of the spine.
He offers me no comment
But greets a dear old friend
Discovered sitting just beyond
On the other side from me.
They chat
And keep at that
For quite some time.
So I redetect the spinal line,
Resume my delicate tracery.
We continue
Along our respective paths
For ten minutes or fifteen.
Then he turns ferocious queen
And asks how I dare take such
Liberties.
"Usually," I say,
"When someone spends so long
Sprawled across my lap,
He wants a spanking,
Long and hard.
But I don't do that crap."

Edmund Miller

AUSTRALIAN RULES

Home for Christmas and looking
for trouble, I spend the idle hours
while the sugarplums are sleeping
spinning the remote control
on my brother's supercolossal,
mythopoetic, cable-connected TV.

He has all those extra channels—
that one from Atlanta
you can never find in the listings
and the fancy ones
you pay extra for
when you have money to burn.

But you keep spinning and spinning.
Nobody ever saw these first-run movies
out in the real world of head-on collisions.
There aren't even any commercials
disengaging you for drift-away.
Even the sex channel is painless.

But Sportschannel, oh you kid!
Who would have thought it? Up
between the antiseptic tennis
and the hoopla of the big-time games,
Australian Rules Football
lacerates the screen.

Dressed for a genteel game of soccer,
red-gold giants baked raw by the sun
explode—with the violence of Rugby—
like fireworks on the Queen's birthday
and thunder across the field getting dirty
down under as they hunger for the goal.

Yet nobody lies bleeding
or gets carried off the field.
And all this without a helmet—
without a kneepad,
without a mask,
without a cup.

Edmund Miller

LEARNING FROM LAP DANCERS
For Rico Brazil at the Show Palace

Earlier in the evening
sitting in the lobby
in all his spandex glory,
so not-on-the-hustle,
so above-it-all,
he looked right through me.
I didn't even know for sure
that he was part of the show.
But then he did get up
to take a turn on stage
and off stage,
and when he made his rounds
and lap-danced over to me,
I could see he could see
that I wanted him
just from the way I was touching.
I tipped him. I tipped him again,
and then he asked,
"Would you like a private show?"
I had the presence of mind
to want to know his price.
But at just twenty dollars,
I had nothing to lose. Semi-private
in a back row, I began licking
his chest—sweet at the belly button,
scented with basil higher up.
I ran hands over his body,
saluting his hardness
with fingertips
When I opened myself
to cockwork invitation,
even half-hard
he filled me up.
But then he unzipped me too
and began jacking my cock.
When in my body worship
almost inadvertently
I glanced a nipple,
with sudden urgency
his cock sprang to full attention.
"So that's the key," I said,

"to ecstasy." So I flicked away
at nipples, and licked away,
paying his price. Just
to finish up I had him turn around
and licked sweat off the hard behind.
Neither of us came. Leaving
me nonetheless light-headed,
he seemed astonished by a ten-dollar tip.
Such open surprise was cheap at the price,
for I saw in a trice
the point of paying twice:
the inaccessible stud
is really yours at last
when he comes to see smiling
as part of the job.

STRANGER

With lushness oozing out of me
like roses from a wound
I round you right with smoke rings
and seduce the air we breathe
describing in particulars
the essence of vermouth.
But then I slowly lose it,
refill my glass with tears
and crowd among the ice cubes
to melt another day.

JOSEPH RATHGEBER

PRIVILEGE

JOSEPH RATHGEBER is a writer and high school English teacher from Clifton, New Jersey. His fiction has been published or is soon to appear in *Fourteen Hills*, *North Dakota Quarterly*, and *Main Street Rag*. His poetry has been published or is forthcoming in *The Literary Review*, the *Quercus Review*, *Hiram Poetry Review*, the *Blue Collar Review*, the *Naugatuck River Review*, *Edison Literary Review*, *Redactions: Poetry & Poetics*, *U.S. 1 Worksheets*, *Poetry South*, and the *Paterson Literary Review*. He is a past nominee for the AWP Intro Journals Project.

Joseph Rathgeber

A DICTIONARY OF THE ENGLISH LANGUAGE

Word is Samuel Johnson liked to inflict pain
on himself.

They found a padlock and duct tape in the back of his armoire.
So he's a masochist: he pandied himself
with the *Book of Common Prayer*
on his backside.

(He called it a *hiney*.)

He occasionally wore a petticoat.
The letter M appeared in his diary entries—
the scholars assume it meant either "masturbation"
or "bowel movement."
They say he died
a virgin.
No hanky-panky
to speak of.

It's hard
to distinguish between Tourette's tics
and self-stimulations.

He supposedly wrote a satire
that wasn't actually a satire
entitled *The Morality of Masochism*—
a work in heroic couplets.
An unexpurgated edition is said to exist
in the annals
of his estate.

Samuel Johnson's safeword was *lexicography*,
a detail which Boswell neglected to mention.

Joseph Rathgeber

YOUNG BLACK MALE

When Tupac rapped *Revenge is like the sweetest joy
next to gettin' pussy*, it was far more jarring
than the preceding line. *I ain't a killer but don't push
me* was pillow soft, boilerplate, a hiccup

in a childhood of abuse. After rape allegations befell
Pac he began to videotape every woman
he fucked saying "I consent to having sex with Tupac
Amaru Shakur" into an RCA camcorder.

These biographical details are complicated by footage
of a teenage Pac as a student at the Baltimore
School for the Arts. He appears flamboyant, tanktopped,
habitually touching fingertips to lips, talking

about being raised by his mother, respecting women,
experiencing rejection because he's "too nice."
His lashes are so long. Other guys "call girls the B-word,"
he says. Pac wrote poetry. *Pac wrote poetry.*

LACAN UNDERSTOOD

Lacan's concepts are too difficult, too dense
to consider, so I have to reconfigure them in poem,
in play. That is, I can dance, yes I can-can,

with 'Can's cons. And I dance scandalously—
petticoat blown open—high kicking my stockings
and skirt skyward. My mirror stage is a recitation

of several bloody Marys in a pitch black public
bathroom. I can define *Gestalt*, but take my meaning
with a grain of salt, a pinch of pepper (too playful).

I have to play with the phallus. I giggle. I get hard.
I suffer a *méconnaissance*. I have to remind myself
that it is not the penis not the penis not the penis.

SHEELA-NA-GIGS

The desks are covered with dicks.

Rocketships, throbbing magic markers,
swollen fingers, dicks dicks dicks.

It's an all-boy school, so what do you expect?

I inspect every desk
at the end of remedial. I erase, rub out,
and efface the penises. It's a futile enterprise:

they keep coming back.

I get proactive.

I combat the penises
with drawings of vaginas:

halved avocados, blooming buds, bouquets.

I include it all: clits, labias majora
and minora, vulval vestibules, mons
pubis, and tufts of pubic hair.

It's art: tastefully rendered.

It's a coterie of sheela-na-gigs carved
into the cornerstones of Irish cathedrals.

Come morning, the entire male
population will be consumed.

FILIAL PIETY

I saw my dad's dick.
Like a strop.
Wiggled and flopped like those salmon swimming upstream
into the furry muzzle of a grizzly bear's mouth.

Mom, startled, leapt backwards against the headboard
as a magician appeared a bouquet from between her legs.

What's left to do?

I got circumcised at eighteen.

Manly (it's my dad's name) never showed me how to keep it clean.
Life is 80 percent maintenance.
An adult body is roughly 70 percent water.

Mom didn't allow rap
with Parental Advisory stickers.

My cassettes were clean radio-friendly versions:
DJ Jazzy Jeff & the Fresh Prince—
I had their whole catalogue.

"Parents Just Don't Understand"
was my joint.

Joseph Rathgeber

HERACLES IN DRAG

Long before Heracles decapitated the head
and cauterized the neck stump of the Hydra,
he was strangling a snake at the foot of his cot
while listening to Lou Reed sing about fellatio.

He carried his olive-wood club like a parasol
and wore his Nemean lion pelt like Venus in furs.
He nursed his wounds with a neti pot and did
his fair share of navel-gazing. It was in bondage

to Queen Omphale that he became a man's man.
She took special note of his nakedness, and when
she hogtied him he became as erect as a Doric column.
He was made into a seamstress and wielded a distaff

and a spindle. He knew, and always used to say,
You have to sashay before you strut. And so every
Liberian rebel tacked Heracles posters to their
bedroom walls. They wore wigs, wedding dresses,

AK-47s, ball gowns, feather boas, sequined purses,
sheer blouses, shower caps, and chanted "sexual
dimorphism isn't destiny" to a staccato beat. They
pressed a branding iron to their flesh spelling HRCLS.

Idolizing a Greek brute from a bygone epoch makes
perfect sense. Picture General Butt Naked in nothing
but his birthday suit and combat boots backed by
a cross-dressing militia. It's violence for any millennium.

NEEDLE WORK

Here I am sitting with my needle work.
And here I am bathing the blinds in the shallow
water of the tub, scrubbing off the matted
dust with a wire brush. My flaxen hair.

Here I am renaming myself Josephine.
I'm proclaiming the name of both my sister
and my most adored shut-in poet to be Emily.
Here I am a schoolteacher, erasing

every penis penciled on every desk
by every pubescent boy—swollen-headed,
erect, veiny—and replacing them with full,
flowering Georgia O'Keefe vagina sketches.

Here I know the two dots atop the Brontë
name is called an umlaut. I bump
my head on the skillet hanging from the pot
rack. Here now I want a fill-in-the-blank

of one's own. I want a rotary telephone.
But I don't want to be a switchboard operator
plugging TRS connectors into rows of female
jacks. No, sir. Her I misspell intentionally.

A margin is much like a hem. Here I have
nothing in my throat. Here I am looking
like a little perverse madonna. Here I am
dying in childbirth. I am a Marian apparition.

THE GAY POETS

I love gay men. Almost as much as I love
Marxists.

Now they're congregating—
not the Marxists, but the gay men.

It's a salon—not beehive, eyebrow threading, mani-, pedi-,
bronzer, the Rachel, feather bangs *salon*—
but salon like wine and cheese,
chitchat,
fainting couches, and cocktails. We're talking

Sarah Lawrence scholars: first-name feminine,
surname masculine. Hosts,
private homes, patrons, and invites-only.

Throw in the occasional handjob.

And the publisher only needs a handshake
and a xerox of the profile in the *Times* to make a contract offer.

Privilege: I'm writing about privilege.

They're well-fed, but remain so thin,
so threadbare it's fashionable:

Is that Fruit of the Loom or chintz?

Clink glasses.

Where are all the gay janitor poets?

The poets with paunches, Carhartts, key rings crammed with keys,
sleeves rolled up past the elbows so as to not get soaked
when snaking toilets.

No janitor poet is getting laid.

No publishers, no patrons of the arts, no GED,
and no union card neither.

Joseph Rathgeber

LYSOL

Lysol is a multipurpose. It's a brand.
It's a household name.
It's under your kitchen sink.

Lysol is a disinfectant. It eliminates odors.

Ladies, you can douche with it—
splash a capful into your cooter
post-coitus.

Incorporate it into your daily routine:
dust, sweep, mop,
and save the sudsy bucket
for that special moment after hubby comes
home from a hard day's work.

Vachel Lindsay chose it as his method
of suicide. He swallowed
an entire bottle of the stuff.

That sissy wanted the easy out.

MY KID

My kid will eat dirt. He will touch pond turtles.
He will pocket a peppermint Binaca bottle and a slim zippo so he can

combine the two elements into a shoddy flamethrower.
He'll be rough-hewn, test batteries on his tongue, and act rambunctious

in the funhouse. My kid will not be called a child—
it's an infantile term and Old Testament biblical. *Kid* is the term—

my kid will be a gutter punk. He'll know how to bore
a hole like a carpenter bee into a plank board. He'll have the know-how

to round corners wide and cure cankersores with saltwater.
He'll butter corncobs with his fork. My kid will tip cattle. He'll tip waitresses

but steal the silverware. He'll snort pixie sticks,
balance spoons on the tip of his nose, and revel in the smell of gasoline.

My kid will find a means to subsist when his world
collapses like wet cardboard at the curb. But for now, my kid's a still sleeper—

he scares the life from me. He's cozied to the crib corner,
belly down. I steady my finger under his nostrils and feel for air.

BILL TRÜB

Memory Hits

BILL TRÜB is a writer and wanderer, having visited more than 30 countries. He holds an MA from Cardiff University in Wales and recently served 16 months as a Peace Corps volunteer in rural South Africa. His poetry and microfiction have been published in six British anthologies and, most recently, in *Sentence: A Journal of Prose Poetics* (Issue 9). Bill is 30, lives in Brooklyn and is ISO MASC. roll-TOP desk 4 LTR.

WORLD WIDE WEB

I.

I know a man with two first names, two last names and 365 different faces. He's building a nitroglycerine bomb he plans to detonate at Machu Picchu. "Do not focus in the destruction," he tells me. "Look, I am creating, no?"

He was multiglacial when we met in a locker room in Caracas. I'd just bench-pressed a set of encyclopedias; he'd carved ice cubes into his abdomen. His smile revealed icicles for incisors. We mangled Spanglish in a jacuzzi for an hour before slinking to the sauna's underbelly. There, I melted him to my size.

We were 27. I told him I was from New York City, which was a lie. He asked me what Americans call people from Venezuela. I said, "Mexicans," and neither of us laughed.

I told him I was the editor of the world's worst business magazine. He told me he was a doctor and that he saved a life last week. I asked if he could save mine.

He pretended to think, slowly shifting shapes. He had a year's worth to choose from.

II.

Balancing on latitudes like tightropes, I searched the planet. When I reached Toronto, the CN Tower fell flaccid. I took twine from my knapsack and continued spinning my web.

Tied an enormous knot around the skyscraper, connected it to a sign marking Bloor Street, unraveled for a mile, made a loop around a flagpole flying the Maple Leaf, meandered through Chinatown, wove the line through a bike rack opposite a Tibetan eatery, crisscrossed it around tree trunks on U of T's campus, bound it to a random statue, then asked a valet at the Hilton to hold the tail end. Tightly.

At 4:25pm, he was snagged. Fidgety, unshaven, surprised to see me. "My dear in headlights," I joked. It had been nearly two years since Caracas.

He took me to a corner café. We traded eyeballs and stared at each other. Far-sighted, the both of us. We spoke in our second languages, resting our mother tongues. He told me who he'd been dating and I acted happy. I told him of my sister's cancer and he promised to steal it.

In his studio on Richmond Street West, he said, "We shouldn't do this" and indented me into the double bed. "Wish we'd never met," I said, unbuttoning his flannel with my right hand, untying our heartstrings with the left.

DRAG

A finger painting he made twenty-five years ago:
a boy, blue face, yellow neck, green smile
waving at an orange house, red dad in the chimney
waving back, purple sun filling the sky...

Tonight, he's trudging through Alphabet City,
the pull of chandeliers, one hung
from each earlobe, pavement scraping
golden arms, clinks of crystals smashing,
pinging into gutters, no cabbies stopping
to haul him to Astoria at this hour.

When the walkabout memory hits, he hoots,
flicks off his stilettos and continues, barefoot,
in the direction of the orange house.

WHAT I DID

Held a conch to my ear
and heard the silk of Etta,
opened a mail bomb
and found a love letter,
peered into a pistol
and saw a barrel of monkeys,
popped a red balloon
and became a terror threat,
sent up a smoke signal
and was texted back,
watched you sleep
and realized all men are afraid.

A SOFTENING OF ARMOR

Born gypsum of Paris, two statues
met and merged in purgatory,
the curtains there are tasteful, sheer
so light can fondle, so skin can breathe
and chip away the castings, simians
now, inhaling the newborn dawn

like fiends, fruitcakes, the ache
for contact, reciprocity a drug
we've all let within, a softening
of armor to embolden the probe
of teeth and knuckles and penis

since we've molted and become
the creatures we were told to hate,
mobile, limb-moshing humans
crackling, entering inch by fat inch

a society of cinders, no blanket,
no water can satisfy this kind
of fervor, triggering wails of warning

when blue at the stem, ripping
through the black hollow,

the bodily core stretching 'til it fits.

SONGBIRD

I know a secret island where a *tan man* wears a *hat*.

In its westernmost village, there's Monster—a drinking hole where real men reel men. Flimsy wrists outnumber clenched fists. Sometimes, the Earth wrenches clockwise and everyone has equal access to its axis.

The crowd is a mixer of young men muscular as grasshoppers and older men in tight Levis flashing bulges—wallets. Every Thursday evening, I enter Monster through its exit, scan the bar and top the nearest stool. I don't order a drink, never dance. Just bird-watch.

He perches, right knee bent, boot flat against a stone wall. He looks old enough to have seen the revolt with his own eyes. Clumps of mascara, a hooked nose. He wears black trousers, a white undershirt and a maroon, double-breasted jacket. Strands of ashen hair are tucked behind his ears.

Moving only his lips, he mouths the lyrics to every song the deejay plays. Eighties synth-hits, saccharine pop from '98, disco diva classics—he says every word without feeling any of them. Sometimes, the mirrorball casts a matrix of stars onto his vacant face. Aimless in ascent, but neither lost nor fading. He'll have his own stories when he lands.

INNOCENT ENGINES

Beyond the brink, drenched,
a glistening glaze slicking
the dark hairs on my chest
and trail, honeycombed,
amorous sludge made by you
for me, solely. Men will come
from distances with wampum
and first-borns, offering lobola
but you're unswayed, steadfast,
committed to the innocent engine
greasy and purring beside you.

THE HUSH

It happens on a May morning.
The grass is dewy like vaginas,
gym class is held outside.

Your instructor rocks a tight buzz cut.
A stopwatch on a cord flirts
with his camouflaged heart.

Ryan edges Randy—no one's surprised.
Keith and Chip run and run and run and
tie. Taylor sprains his ankle.

You race the nameless kid
who wishes you luck, then beats you.
Your buddies bust their bellies and die
laughing.

"Newman," Tully says. "That homo
made you his bitch!" They heckle like jackals
into the locker room.

The kid with motor legs
faces a corner, changes his shorts.
You creep up.

The hush.

A semicircle forms.

The kid turns.

He knows.

Seconds stumble.

You think, "Good race,"
but say, "Fucking fag."
And you know he won because he's used to being chased.

THE UNSPEAKABLE

Fourteen years and two days ago, I asked my uncle
to explain the difference between nightmares and dreams.
"Depends how tough you are," he said, kissing my ankle.
My calf, kneecap. His tongue, a trout curling upstream.

"Tough guys don't have nightmares." The fish hit my lips, guardians
of the unspeakable. He bent me. "Tough guys don't squeal like pigs."
"I'm tough, I won't." My bedroom became a toxic garden.
Killer bees stabbed our shadows, the canopy fell, twigs
swelled into a roof-busting family tree with a wholesome trunk
and queer branches. After forever, he removed his stinger.

It stunk.
Its musk lingered.

He cupped my tears in his palms, splashed them on his face. "See!
No monsters in here," he said and went to fetch warm milk for me.

BATHTUB

The faucet slams a rope
of water into the porcelain basin.
I step in, let the rush overtake my toes
and crest at my shinbones.

I squat, submerge myself.
Some cold front, some Arctic blast
ushers December inside,
seats him in my lap.

My kneecaps become ice caps
above the surface, frozen
to thawing thighs beneath.

Follow the slopes south
to the patch of black sea grass.
Find the only thing alive in this ocean:

the electric eel
stabbing up through the current,
abuzz with manifesto, so proud
of its voltage.

When the tide turns, grab hold.
It will shock you.

COME OUT

Hung on hangers, an urge
propels us out and over thresholds
into city streets without signs.
Gales blow back our hoods.

Someone who knows something—
a cipher, the address—howls, *Walk
to the first zebra crossing, turn right,
continue straight, you'll see a McDonalds...*

Directions, lost beneath blusters.
Somewhere, four walls twiddle,
an enveloping woman readies
a kettle, a sachet of chai. A bed
and its duvet will understand.

In a vacant lot we're spun, scarves
unraveling, cheeks snow-slapped.
We duck into a phone booth,
press all the buttons, but none
launches us to the shelter

hoping to greet us, as is,
no questions asked except,
"What color is your word?"

THAT GUY

When I took my first guitar lesson I'd just sprouted pubes and learnt to waste semen. Calluses crowned my fingertips, yet my teacher said I didn't practice enough. I wasn't sure if he meant strumming or coming. Nonetheless, I memorized Bon Jovi chords six days a week. On Sundays, I attended catechism class. Whenever I sneezed, a chorus chimed *God Bless You!* "Yeah, right," I thought, "*as if Zeus has time for bootlickers or likes being called Jupiter. He must hate being hounded: 'Hey, aren't you that guy from that myth?'*"

Allergic to churches and bored of frets, I continued masturbating. My hands softened again. I felt no guilt. Gentle barbarians set quiet wildfires in my head. I thought clearly. I trapped air in my belly and floated everywhere.

I miss that guy. I wish he'd never begun skating the fringes, outlying for thrills. Letting the grey wind whistle through his whiskers. Having flings with exotic places, long-term relations with dull jobs. Clipping coupons, uncovering bones, sugarcoating. Acquiring a staring problem, mistaking people for peepholes and trying to see through them. He wanted it all but didn't have anywhere to put it.

DAVID POSEIDON

He loves running from the tide,
spittle awash in whiskey and the dead hum
of cop cars underwater, a siren song.

Baby bullet exited his skull's ceiling,
a blowhole for daydreams to float out,
alongside plankton and flashbacks.

He's a slave to the Atlantic, the way
it sways its hips, how it swallows all.
He worships warships, counts sand.

There are sea ballerinas, delicate
as tiptoes, pirouetting to heartbeats,
ripping open their fuchsia gills

to invite him inside. But he ocean-crawls
with hermit crabs, shell-shocked. Sorry, girls.
He's busy. He's drowning. He has somewhere to be.

STEVE TURTELL

DELICATE BAYS

STEVE TURTELL was born in Brooklyn and lives in New York City. He was director of public programs at the Museum of the City of New York, the South-Street Seaport Museum, and the New-York Historical Society. His 2001 chapbook, *Letter to Frank O'Hara*, was the 2010 winner of the Rebound Chapbook Prize given by Seven Kitchens Press and was reissued with an introduction by Joan Larkin in 2011. His work has been published in numerous periodicals and the anthologies *Blood And Tears: Poems For Matthew Shepard* (Painted Leaf Press, 1999), *This New Breed: Bad Boys, Gents And Barbarians II* (Windstorm Creative, 2001), and *Collective Brightness: LGBTIQ Poets on Faith, Religion & Spirituality* (Sibling Rivalry Press, 2011).

www.steveturtell.com

ST. FRANCIS' SOLILOQUY
for Claire Daly

One day, you will be as naked as an animal.
Let that day come before you die.

The wolf will be your friend when you are no longer a wolf.
When you no longer flee from God, birds will no longer flee from you.

They will sit on your shoulder and listen to your song,
your soul's steady hum.

The lion will welcome you into his pride and rest at your feet.
The peacock will be eager to stand with you.

When you no longer pose in furs and feathers, stealing
a glory that isn't yours, all glory will be revealed.

When you leave this world the world comes back to you.
And the world will teach you how to love.

Let God pour in.
Then give it all back.

Steve Turtell

ORPHAN
for Joan Larkin

My mother is dead.
I'm glad.
I was a good son.

My mother is gone.
I'm sad.
I was in love with her.

My mother loved me.
It hurt.
She loved my brother more.

My mother hated me.
I learned.
She had no one else to punish.

My mother ignored me.
I yearned.
My soul stretched all the way to God.

POEM IN FOUR QUESTIONS
(Written After Making Love to
One Man While Thinking of Another)
For DF and SM

What will I do with this love
    That you don't want?

What will I do with this love
    That you don't need?

What will I do with this love
    That you can't use?

What will I do with this love
    That I can't keep?

Steve Turtell

LETTER TO FRANK O'HARA

It had been raining for ten years—
just after our vows too, when the life
of the party shouted "Drop dead."
What aplomb! All those faithless Springs
suddenly worthless. Years of abandonment
counting for nothing. Oh horrors of
enchantment, beauty of truculence.
You can always depend upon the hostility of lovers
But we, a glamorous, shuddering chorus,
eyes averted, move *en pointe* past
the confessional's lurid glow,
that peep-show of self-pity. Really, Mary!

As if our holy yawns don't prove
we're simply riddled with purity
and will float softly, silently
as the dreams of inconsolable rhinoceri,
pitiable as the tears of lost seagulls,
sure as Adam's apple pie, straight to heaven.
The angels' impatience says we've
all prayed for too little and they
can't wait to scold us. God's redecorating.
He wants all his darlings back.

Oh Frank. Have you missed us terribly,
whom you never met? I picture your daily
grand jeté over the sun, knowing the moon
never tires of loving you. I long to change
costumes and visit. Let's see. Blandishments,
pitchforks, foreskins. Well! But then Edward
told me you had the longest he'd ever seen.
My mother loved me so I got to keep mine,
ensuring that there I would always be a goy.
Just knowing that I've kissed lips that once
kissed yours—but enough. Discretion is
the better part of careerism. Now there
is only one poet I love to read while dreaming.

IN PRAISE OF CONCRETE
Homage to Allen Ginsberg

The wonders of concrete I sing,
demanding shoe-sole devourer, ground of dangerous adolescent adventures
    down any and all unknown paths,
        smasher of dropped eggs and ripe peaches,
        scraper of knees and elbows, smotherer of weedlots, protector of ants
        eternal enemy of the moist, dark, uncovered earth.

Concrete you are the end of eras,
herald of decades, augur of change from muted summer paths
    of nineteenth-century childhoods
    onto you, solid foundation of the twentieth century,
    domain of roller skates, bikes
    and juvenile delinquents, beautiful canvas of urban dreams, mixing chalk,
    spit, coffee, and blackened gum onto city-large Pollocks revised daily by millions.

Without you there'd be no Skulsees, no Hopscotch,
no curbs & fire-hydrants & hole-punched-girders bearing traffic signs,
    no silver octagonal columns rising from pyramidal bases of
    poured, rounded squares of you.

Concrete! Trundled from site to site in elephant-colored bomb-shaped trucks,
    or mixed on the spot, your fat rivers of rough green batter pouring
    into sidewalk molds, sprinkled with pebbles like rock-sugar streusel
    of green & black & scratched-silver & chalk-
    white nuts, edges beveled with serrated-edged trowels held in thick
    muscled forearms emerging from rolled flannel sleeves, arms with
    milky green-gray splotches, speckled and
    matted with miniature hair-pulling nuggets.

Concrete how prolific you are!
    Producer of fortunes small and large, generator of loose change for
    low-level gangsters and brutally talented thugs who parlay a minor
    craft into major wrought-iron fenced and red-bricked mansions
    in the delicate bays of Long Island's north shore, the green recesses
    of upstate New York and the horsey hills lying all unsuspected behind
    the clever camouflage of industrial New Jersey.

Concrete, you are immense
    with your black lightning cracks, your white panels home to galaxies
    of blackened bubble gum, grass-sprouting slits, crevasses, miniature
    plateaus and ravines, the treacherous landscape of all creatures who

live on or near you, the ants who emerge from your damp caves to
walk upside down on cantilevered cliffs, or the prowling tomcats
whose fierce amber eyes and midnight-sure paws, ignore your
beautiful irregularities.

Oh concrete, the water streams endlessly down on you,
    the oil-rainbowed rivers carrying bottlecaps and gum rappers and ice-
    cream stick rafts to clogged sewers, the black rain of cities turning
    your fat grey pebbles a majestic purple, spit-shining your neighboring
    squares of slate to blue-grey patten-leather.

Concrete I love you in the summer
    when the heat shimmers above you. I love your salt-stained endurance
    of winter and the urban cool of your springs and autumns. Concrete
    you are mysterious as glass, more durable than glazed tile, noble
    as marble, a worthy substance, deserving of praise.
    And next I'll sing of your beautiful sister Tar, and after that,
    the wonders, far surpassing the antique, pastel beauties
    of dull country roads and monotonous rural scenery,
    the wonders of all city streets.

THE SUBSTANCE OF JOY
Johannes Vermeer At The National Gallery

A cautious friendliness prevails.
Strangers smile sweetly;
apologize when passing.

We all gawk at
"The Girl with the Wineglass."
A few risk comments.

Her smile, tulip red dress, the blue-gold
'harlequin' tiled floor—get more
and less informed notice.

I look at the cordial glass
—precarious between
finger and thumb, and her grin,

not yet slack. A dandified,
self-styled "connoisseur"
sweeps by. Dark fedora,

mauve brocaded-satin scarf,
camel-hair coat, cordovan wingtips
—all gorgeous, elegant. His hauteur

alone worth the effort of some
painter or other—Whistler
in a very bad mood?

The comments die down
around him. Why embarrass
ourselves when all we want

is pleasure, and pictures of it?
After he's gone I say to my neighbor,
"She looks drunk." He considers,

shrugs before backing out.
The three-deep crowd surges
ever so politely forward.

It's difficult to get close

to the paintings; but not
as difficult as painting them

with such unwieldy tools:
soft mounds of oily pigment
spread in blending rivulets;

the oddly shaped knife;
tiny thatches of sable
carefully bound to thin sticks;

the camera obscura Vermeer
peered through at lovely women,
at the ample room with a few props

—the wall map weighted
with iron-blue dowel,
a table, a leaded window

filled with the famous light
he lured onto his canvas.
Centuries later, we too love

what he so clearly saw:
thin red gleams on parted lips,
a liquid, white slice of teeth,

thick rugs bunched like
pantaloons on the waxed table,
the shimmering folds of lemon

souffle gowns, caressed by
the same sun that shone on you,
now shining on us, on the intricate

smears encrusting the linen
canvas, all that remains of
the substance of your joy.

OCEAN VUONG

Self-Portrait with Exit Wounds

Ocean Vuong was born in Saigon, Vietnam. He is the author of the chapbook *Burnings* (Sibling Rivalry Press, 2010) and recently graduated from Brooklyn College, CUNY. He was the winner of the 2012 Stanley Kunitz Memorial Prize from *American Poetry Review*, a semi-finalist for the 2011 Crab Orchard Series in Poetry First Book Award, and was a recipient of an Academy of American Poets Award and the Connecticut Poetry Society's Al Savard Award. His poems appear in *RHINO*, *diode*, *Guernica*, *Drunken Boat*, *South Dakota Review*, and *PANK*, among others.

www.oceanvuong.blogspot.com

Ocean Vuong

THE SEVENTH CIRCLE OF EARTH

On April 27, 2011, a gay couple was found burned to death in their home in Dallas, Texas.

-Dallas Voice, *April 2011*

So much went wrong
   and still we danced—as if inside us
     a terrible flower was waiting

to be crushed. Now this house,
   as we knew it would, is burning.
     Torches rain like fragments

from a shattered star.
   Their eyes glistening through
     the heat's warped rise.

Let them see us, framed
   through what's left of windows,
     the way we expire—

fingers relearning collarbone
   for the last time, shoulders
     wrapped in this throne

of arms interlocked, the pictures
   we hung bursting into golden blossoms
     of memory. Don't laugh—

I burn happiest when haloed
   with your scent, wreathed
     in the vestiges of your fading.

The beams starting to crack now.
   Don't laugh—just tell me the story
     again, of the finches who flew

from burning Jerusalem,
   how they hurled such bright wings
     against the wind for fragments

of flight. And how ruin nested
   in their throats until their cries
      dwindled to a thread of smoke

unraveling into sky. Speak—
   until your voice is no more
      than the crackling of charred

bones. Until your name masters
   my mouth and flames singe shut
      the jaw's exigence

to sing. Love, quick, love me
   anyway. Don't laugh. The walls
      are crumbling. Don't laugh

when they search the cinders
   and find a flower—a rose,
      a pansy crisped to ash

when it's only my tongue.
   My tongue crumbling
      in my husband's mouth—

IN THE TIME OF HURRICANES

He takes the boy's hand
and they step into the storm.
Wind twisting every tree
into a god. No one left to witness
the fracture—or glory in their dance.
The street starting to flood.
Water above their ankles, drowning
the flaws in their clumsy waltz.
Carefully, he dips the boy backward
until the world appears changed.
A few strands of hair graze
the rising river, and he thinks
everything lost can be salvaged
with only enough desperation.
That to gather what's left of happiness
is a triumph equal to hearing his name
arrive inside a softer mouth.
When the nearest birch shatters,
raking the sky with its fall, the boy,
startled, looks into his eyes
for the first time—and this,
he thinks, is proof
he has prayed correctly.

ONCE

Brooklyn's too cold tonight
even for the most desperate.
You want to believe

the steam jeweled on every
lit window—a sign
of two voices, speaking low

and not the heat
of someone waiting
for reasons.

The blond boy
is walking towards you
like a knife, an echo sharpened

with what it touched.
If only you could test
the pavement with your

knees, ask him to spare you
your name made new
in his mouth. If only

you are not already
wounded. But too late:
his jaw emerges

from the shroud of smoke
and you're reaching beneath
your shirt, making sure

there's still one more
warm place
to enter—

ON FALLING

Beneath the orchard's shadowed bruising,
        where only the wind can find their lips,
two boys kneel at the foot of a tree

as faithful children would genuflect
        before the world's final shrine.
Below the waist, the fly's dark slit

is a wound. The air inside warmer
        than a hundred hallelujahs.
And the apples, weary of their weight, have begun

to drop, starlight dashed across their sheen
        as each sphere falls closer
to October. What else in the sound of fruit

turning to thunder, but the root aching
        to reclaim what it surged, how the gift
glistening at the furthest bough beckons

the hand into orbit. What else but the earth
        pulling these boys into themselves,
their moon-blessed backs slick

with sweet rot. What else but nothing.
        Nothing—because the body, in aching,
will find a way. Because the body, in aching, knows

that skin is but a temporary border,
        that gravity is the only
unbroken promise.

BROTHER

The poison failed at first.

When mother forgot
and began to hum a cheery tune,
he writhed inside her—

his hands, small blossoms
scraping the darkening world
she carried.

The morning he stilled
to a cool pit, they slaughtered a hen
to urge the spirit onward.

It rained for days. Rain
igniting father's face
tilted skyward.

Rain drowning the lilies
where mother knelt and begged
for the butcher's boot

when the headless thing
thrashing in the mud
wouldn't stop

                      raging with questions—

DEVOTION

Instead, the year begins
    with my knees
scraping the hardwood,
    another man trembling
inside this mouth. Fresh snow
    crackling on the window,
each flake a god I've shut out
    for good. Because
the difference between prayer
    and pleasure—is how you move
the tongue. I press mine
    to the navel's familiar
whorl, those dark threads
    descending towards
devotion. And there's nothing
    more holy than holding
a man's heartbeat between
    your teeth—sharpened
with want. This mouth the last entry
    into January: this hunger, this
muted scream silenced
    at last, with a grenade
of white flowers. Fresh snow
    crackling on the window
and so what—if my feathers
    are burning. Even
with wings, the stars are still
    too far away.

Ocean Vuong

SELF-PORTRAIT WITH EXIT WOUNDS
Củ Chi, Viet Nam

Instead, let it be the echo to every prayer
drowned out by rain, cripple the air

like a name flung inside a sinking boat,
let it shatter the bark on the nearest kapok

and through it, beyond the jungle's lucent haze,
the rot and shine of a city trying to forget

the bones beneath its sidewalks, through
the refugee camp sick with smoke and half-sung

hymns, the shack lit with the final candle, the blackened
faces we held between our hands and mistook

for brothers, let it past the wall, into a room brightened
with snow, a room furnished only with laughter,

Wonder Bread and mayonnaise raised
to cracked lips as testament to a triumph

no one recalls, let it brush against the new-born's
flushed cheek as he's lifted in his father's palms

wreathed with fishgut and cigarettes,
burrow through that wall where a yellow boy

soaks in blue television flood, the boy
who cheers as each brown gook crumbles

on the screen where Vietnam burns perpetually
in the mind's blown fuse, let it whisper

in his ear—before sliding through, clean
like a promise, and pierce the painting of fruit

above the bed, enter the cold supermarket
where a Hapa woman wants to shout

Father! at every white man possessing
her nose, may it sing, briefly, inside

her mouth, before laying her down between
the jars of tomato and blue boxes of pasta,

the deep red apple rolling from her palm,
let it drill a hole in her throat and into

the prison where a father watches
the moon until he's convinced it's the last wafer

God refused him, and let it enter the wood
where a man is slumped at a desk lit only

with night's retreat, trying to forge an answer
out of ash pressed into words, may it crack

that stubborn bone above his heart—blood
and blood seeping through an epic

of blank pages, but if for nothing else, let it soar
like a kiss we've forgotten how to give

one another, slicing through all the burning rooms
we've mistaken for childhood, and may it go on

to circle the earth, warping through seasons
and years before slamming back into 1968,

to Hong Long Bay: the sky replaced
with fire, the sky only the dead look up to,

may it find my grandfather, crouched beside
the Army Jeep, his blond hair flickering

in naplam-blasted wind, pin him
down to the dust, where mother and I

will crawl out from history, that wreck
of shadows, tear open his olive fatigues

and clutch that name hanging from his neck,
that name we press to our tongues as if to relearn

the word for *live*, let us carry him home on our backs,
bathe his cooling body in salt and jasmine and call it

good, but if for nothing else, let me believe
as I weave this death-beam like a blind woman

stitching a flap of skin to her daughter's ribs,
let me believe I was born for this—as I cock back

the chamber, smooth and slick, like a true
Charlie. Like I could hear the song drowned out

by rain as I lower myself between the sights
and pray—that nothing moves.

FAKING IT

At breakfast—his parents asked
about the noise. Told them
he had been crying all night.
The slow nods. Silence broken
with spoons. Anything
to save them, he thought,
from knowing the other
shadow breathing beneath
his sheets, that their only son
found pleasure lighting
himself on fire.

NOEL DEAN DOSS

THE EMBRACE

NOEL DEAN DOSS attained a Bachelor's Degree in Art at West Texas A&M and graduated from Colorado Institute of Art, Denver. Coming to art later in life, he was inspired by painting and drawing classes he took at SACI in Florence, Italy. He works in acrylic, oils, pencils, collage, and anything with which he can experiment. He loves finding new materials and combining traditional ones. He likes to take the viewer out of the mundane by sometimes raw and shocking ways. His work has been exhibited in the Green Room at Twiggs in San Diego, California, and the Leslie Lohman Annex in New York City.

SUBMIT TO ASSARACUS

The mission of Sibling Rivalry Press is to develop, publish, and promote outlaw artistic talent—those projects which inspire people to read, challenge, and ponder the complexities of life in dark rooms, under blankets by cell-phone illumination, in the backseats of cars, and on spring-day park benches next to people reading Adrienne Rich. We encourage submissions to *Assaracus* by gay male poets of any age, regardless of background, education, or level of publication experience. Submissions are accepted during the months of January, May, and September. For more information, visit us online.

SUBSCRIBE TO ASSARACUS

Readers can subscribe to receive a year of *Assaracus*. The subscription price is $50.00 for U.S. readers and $80.00 for international readers (including shipping), which buys you four book-length (120+ pages), perfect-bound issues of our grand stage for gay contemporary poetry. Subscriptions are available through our website.

NEW FROM SIBLING RIVALRY PRESS

Butcher's Sugar by Brad Richard. With a beauty purged of sweetness, the voices of *Butcher's Sugar* sing of the sublime in the debased, violence and desire, the truth of whatever is "rank with the carcass of mystery." Moving from childhood through adulthood, these poems re-inhabit and reclaim myths about the body and the self.

Less Fortunate Pirates: Poems from the First Year Without My Father by Assaracus Editor Bryan Borland. On December 20, 2009, ten days after giving Bryan $1,000.00 to found Sibling Rivalry Press, Jimmy Borland died in a car accident. The poems of *Less Fortunate Pirates* were written during the year that followed and are a love letter from son to father.

Things Said in Dreams by Matthew Temple. Terrorized by her high school classmates, she now has the chance to save their lives. Matthew Temple's *Things Said in Dreams*, the first novel from Sibling Rivalry Press, gives us a female Holden Caulfield and a haunting, memorable story of twisted, dangerous grace.

www.siblingrivalrypress.com

CPSIA information can be obtained at www.ICGtesting.com
Printed in the USA
LVOW080236230213

321417LV00002B/61/P